THE ART OF
Balancing

LANE CARNES

Copyright © 2024 Lane Carnes.

All rights reserved. No part of this book may be reproduced, stored, or transmitted by any means—whether auditory, graphic, mechanical, or electronic—without written permission of both publisher and author, except in the case of brief excerpts used in critical articles and reviews. Unauthorized reproduction of any part of this work is illegal and is punishable by law.

ISBN: 978-1-63950-226-4 (sc)
ISBN: 978-1-63950-227-1 (e)

This publication contains the opinions and ideas of its author. It is intended to provide helpful and informative material on the subjects addressed in the publication. The author and publisher specifically disclaim all responsibility for any liability, loss, or risk, personal or otherwise, which is incurred as a consequence, directly or indirectly, of the use and application of any of the contents of this book.

Writers Apex

Gateway Towards Success

8063 MADISON AVE #1252
Indianapolis, IN 46227
+13176596889
www.writersapex.com

CONTENTS

Dedication v
Gravel Meditations 1
Montaigne and Consciousness 7
Virtuous Living 10
Locke and American Politics 13
Baldwin and Race 17
Existentialism and the Pandemic 20
Waves of the Same Sea 24
The Pope and Gang Violence in Central America 27
The Soullessness of the Church 29
The Toxicity of the Pandemic Within Academia 33
Financial Freedom and Dickinson's Poetry 36
Titanium Plates and Impressionism 40
Cycling and Right Thinking 45
To Write or Not to Write 48
Deconstruction of the Breath 51
Musings on Checkmate 54
Stagnated Loss of Curiosity 57
Eliminating Poverty 62
Sandra and Toulouse-Lautrec 66
Running Transforms 69
Juárez and Immigration 72
Michelangelo's Depiction of the Soul 75
Financial Security and Klimt 79
Creating and Nervous Fatigue 84

Russell's Affection 89
The Aging Athlete Gliding on Gravel 91
Art as a Conduit for God 96
Self-discovery 99
The Dichotomy of El Salvador's Coffee Bean 101
A Missed Opportunity for Diplomatic Unity and Cooperation 104
Guatemala Sold Its Agricultural Soul 108
The Honduran Enigma Baffles the U.S. 113
Austin's Forgotten Diplomacy 116
Suffering and Paradoxical Thinking 119
The Ego and Love Conundrum 122
Conversations Drinking Café Yaucono on a Saturday 124
American Corona Beer Attitude and Diplomacy 128
Blacks Enslaved Blacks Before Being Shipped to America ... 131
America's Indifference 134
Biden's Catastrophic Withdrawal From Afghanistan 137
French Avarice Is the Culprit of Haiti's Failed State 140
America's Brothel House in Cuba 144
Debt, Excessive Procreation and Indecision Are Ruinous ... 148
Treasuring Enthusiasm and Solitude 151
The Mirrored Failure of Vietnam in Afghanistan 154
Pedal Strokes on Rural Roads 158
Constable's Canvas and Two White Cats 160
The U.S. Loses Its Global Credibility as a Beacon of Democracy ... 163
Goya's Dark Genius 172
Sports, Politics and the Art of War 176
Religious Services Lack Sustenance 180
The Art of Balancing in an Inattentive and Divided World 183
Final Rumination 188

DEDICATION

I dedicate *The Art of Balancing* to the freedom and liberty afforded to all citizens born in the United States of America and other countries of the free world. There is an existential crisis encroaching upon people's separate and collective lives. Many authors choose to write to gain fame or to be recognized on a bestseller's list for others to read of their "encapsulated formulas" for solving life's most difficult questions.

My desire is to deconstruct the purpose of composing the written word, not so much to attract a plethora of followers but to sit still long enough in a form of meditation and self-examination of my uniqueness within the context of the spiritual, philosophical and political imbroglio of man's existence with himself and others.

Most people search for meaning following Robert Frost's advice of traversing down the least-travelled road diverging in the forest along with the one most often taken. I choose neither one of these "expressways" as I create a path, which is distinctively my own, in the human macrocosm that entices man to adopt the ideas of others at the expense of his own. Unless a person takes the time to tailor his own gateway, he will never find significance or a clear intention in being because he has ignored the inherent calling of his individual soul.

Be bold and fearless in finding the truth God wants each member of the "global neighborhood" to determine for him/herself in the confusion of living.

GRAVEL MEDITATIONS

IT WAS DECEMBER 1, 2019 on a 56-mile training bike ride when the front wheel of Rafael's black and white Trek Speed Madone found some fine gravel and slid from under him on Old Settler's Way, a rural road about 18.5 miles east of Cibolo, Texas just north of San Antonio. It was a route he was very familiar with since he normally rode it several times a month. The main attraction out there was that there was very little traffic on those country byways.

This was a turn in which Rafael would usually cut the corner due to the rarity of vehicular activity, but on this afternoon, a vehicle was traveling down the road. There was a stop sign for the approaching car, so Rafael took a 90 degree turn at a moderate speed and that's all he remembered.

Triathlons and writing were passions that Rafael enjoyed now for approximately 28 years. Sports was an activity consuming much of his youthful years growing up in San Juan, Puerto Rico. The countless hours playing basketball and running track and cross country filled his days as an adolescent. Eventually, running became his preferred sport when he moved to Texas to attend college. The cross training involved in triathlons (swimming, biking and running) became appealing to him as the years of the repetitiveness of pounding the road from only running wore on his body and soul.

Life is a balancing act where a person is forced to remain on a seesaw on a never-ending motion of ups and downs. The ocean serves as a perfect metaphor for this as the constant flow of the waves rolling on to the shore continues indefinitely. The countless views of the beach filled Rafael's repertoire of memories from the mild waves of Piñones roaring on the rock formations and the large shallow pool of salt water created behind its solid wall in el Viejo San Juan to the enormous waves curling over the deep blue Caribbean Sea as they tumbled towards the Spanish fort El Morro built in the sixteenth century on the northeastern coast of Puerto Rico.

The writer, much like an athlete who schedules time to train, must carve out some space to sit, meditate and write. Days can slip away as people become involved in the numerous activities that consume their waking hours: work, attending to relationships, maintaining the home, preparing meals, etc. The body requires movement, and the mind must be fed by thoughts. However, each individual soul must be nourished. Education can help a student to think, but he must be careful not to parrot the thoughts of others. Socrates says, "Know yourself," but as a free thinker, everyone should question these types of maxims.

Rafael wanted to become his own architect, and he desired to accomplish this by living his own life purposefully. By this he meant to create his own work of art by crafting his poetry and meditations in prose in books to be read and shared with others but, more importantly, for his own existential ruminations. Much like *Don Quixote de la Mancha*, the first modern novel ever written in the seventeenth century by Miguel de Cervantes, Cervantes was compelled to muse and redact his own quixotic view of the world based primarily on his experiences. Many university scholars only focus their research on famous literature, such as that written by Cervantes, for example, but Rafael was not interested on dwelling and drooling over the great works of classical writers over the centuries but rather on drafting his own work.

Society does not encourage individuals to think for themselves but rather to absorb the ideas passed down to them through education.

Meditating as prescribed by the Buddha is important and necessary for existence, since inhaling and exhaling air is essential for living. The word of God was breathed into man as described in Genesis. But accepting, believing and practicing these truths were not enough for Rafael. He knew he could not be totally reliant on institutions, like the Church, the state and schools, to do the thinking for him.

Like Ralph Waldo Emerson who dictated the maxim "to rely on yourself," a person must take it a step further by questioning and examining these philosophical viewpoints individually as Emerson did. Poets, like Robert Frost, created their own roads and diverged along the ones less traversed. But an individual should not settle for their roads and adventures. It's imperative for him to deconstruct the thoughts of the classics to construct his work and destiny as a thinker. It is not enough to just "travel the road less travelled," but to embark on painting new roads that still are yet to be born or perceived. The purpose is not to influence or convince others of someone else's observations, but it is an obligation he owes to himself to live with a determined intent and convictions of his own.

Rafael and his wife Josefina spent the weekend in Chicago. Josefina was attending a conference for the Endocrine Society of Medicine. She was kind of like a renaissance woman, in Rafael's mind, because she was interested in so many things. Josefina grew up in Saint Bernard Parish, Louisiana, just outside of New Orleans. She was the third oldest in a family of seven siblings. Her father was an airplane mechanic who maintained those small airplanes that land in the water, and her mother was a nurse who was also knowledgeable in herbal medicine. Her younger sister Anastasia married and moved to Phoenix, Arizona and had three wonderful kids with her husband. Josefina's older sister and four brothers all remained in New Orleans and the surrounding metropolitan area.

In high school Josefina was voted the most popular and social student of the year. She was an athlete on the softball, tennis and basketball teams. In addition, she was a member of the archery club and honor society. She also was a flag girl for the band. She attended the University of Loyola in Louisiana and North Texas State and became a nurse. While working full-time as a nurse, she was accepted to medical school. Josefina graduated from LSU with a medical degree. Her brothers did not attend college, but both of her sisters did. Josefina was the only one in her family who travelled to Europe after graduating from high school, and she became fluent in German. She lived and worked in Germany for about two years after becoming a doctor. Josefina also enjoyed dancing tango and salsa, and she loved learning languages. Rafael never met anyone so well-rounded, intelligent and curious about everything.

In Chicago Rafael ran six miles one day and 11 miles the next along the trail paralleling the Michigan Lake. It was in the 30s outside but sunny, which made it bearable. Josefina ran about two miles and walked for another three perusing the city. One afternoon they visited the Chicago Museum of Modern Art. There they scrutinized the famous water lilies by Monet. Rafael learned that Monet continued to paint in his later years even when he was beginning to go blind. He was fascinated by artists who continue performing their craft until the very end. It seems like each individual has choices to make as he ages. Society often inculcates people with the idea of retirement being a time for relaxing and sitting in a lounge chair on some pristine beach drinking a piña colada and soaking up the sun. But this is a fairytale that leads to stagnation and early decay.

Retirement can become a grind as a person tries to fill his time with activities. For the artist or writer, who has always painted or written, it's essential for him to evolve in his work in order to progress and move forward. There is always a form of resistance at the dawn each morning: to sleep a little longer, to exercise and read a little less and to spend more idle time in front of the T.V. The artist like an aging athlete learns to push through this intransigence as a daily habit and exercise. Monet like many other artists like Van Gogh must have loved the changes of light throughout the day. Light becomes the medium for painting the different perspectives of a water lily or a starry night. The shades created by the trees, shrubbery and the divergent colors of flowers and plants are the tools used by the artist for expressing himself on a canvas. For the writer, it becomes essential to look within to write something original and impactful for the reader but, more importantly, for the growth of his own soul.

Rafael observed the "soul" of the medical profession as he witnessed his sister Rebecca wither away physically after a parathyroid removal that kept her bedridden for two weeks in the hospital and then for another two years in a rehabilitation center. The medical services are so specialized and compartmentalized like so many other institutions in America like schools and government. The doctors took care of the calcium and phosphorous levels affecting Rebecca's kidneys, which is important. But exercise and movement are not a priority. It's true Rebecca was not in very good physical condition before her surgery, but it worsened after the operation.

Physical therapists spent most of their time preparing Rebecca to get into a car from a wheelchair and out of bed from the same mobile device. She had difficulty with balance before surgery because she was about 50 lbs. overweight, but now she was confined to a walker and wheelchair. When Rafael came by to visit and walk Rebecca at the hospital, the nurses immediately indicated that she was too much of a risk to fall for her to walk. After his insistence, one of the nurses ambulated Rebecca with a belt strapped around her waist to grab onto with the aid of the walker.

It was disheartening for Rafael to see his sister's deterioration, much of it brought on by her mental illness and the endless amounts of antipsychotic medications she had been prescribed over the years. She suffered from the diagnosis of manic depression. Our society wants to medicate any type of disorder, and little is done to address the disease of the soul, which all humans suffer from.

Life is a balancing act between ups and downs that everyone experiences. The educational system fails to address the hard facts of life like loss and death that affect every person. Many teachers are parrots of academia passing down superficial data they've learned to their students. Yes, everyone needs to learn that 2+2= 4 and that photosynthesis is important for plants to grow and produce oxygen. But teachers never ask themselves the real questions about life; therefore, students aren't asked these questions either. Of course, man wouldn't be able to survive without photosynthesis. But how does this ability to breathe affect his emotional, psychological and spiritual being? Each person must explore these answers individually. There is not one totally correct answer. It's essential to dwell in the uncertainty of an individual's responses and conclusions.

There is an endless plethora of books written on happiness and the meaning of life. It's necessary to read these books, but then a person should define beatitude, sadness and the meaning of his existence for himself. When a child draws a flower or a dog, what does that figure mean to him? The rose or the tulip expresses its essence through its array of vibrant colors sustained by the sunlight, water and carbon dioxide. Human beings subsist from the oxygen produced by plants, and the body needs water in order to function. The sun also provides the body with vitamin D. There is a coexistence between plants and humans. However, the petals of flowers wilt just as humans eventually become frail and die. So, the fundamental question becomes: What is the significance of living if all life ends in death? This is something everyone must ask himself, and teachers should have these conversations with their students. It's nihilistic to depend on teachers, priests, philosophers, politicians, psychiatrists or any other well-known writer to answer these queries for each individual. It's imperative to read several points of view on this subject, but the perspectives of others should be a springboard for man's own thoughts and opinions. Society is leaving these types of interrogations unanswered.

MONTAIGNE AND CONSCIOUSNESS

MICHEL DE MONTAIGNE, the French philosopher and writer from the sixteenth century, "dedicated himself to the freedom of the mind and peacefulness of the soul," which became his personal foundation for cultivating and educating himself through his writings. "Since philosophy had failed to determine a secure path to happiness, [Montaigne] committed each person to do so in his own way." Rafael agreed with Montaigne that each person should write to sculpt out his individual path if he chooses to write. The ivory towers of academia dedicate their efforts to document and analyze the classics of Shakespeare, Homer, Dante and others, but it is actually more important for each individual to create and redact his own personal classicism. In today's world, the majority of the population allow the news and social media, politicians, the latest technological gadgets and academic professors to guide and define their thinking. Most people believe what they hear on the news without questioning the information they absorb. Just look around while at any airport and notice the numbness of people mindlessly connected to their android phones, tablets and computer screens. Go through the bookstores and notice the number of books dedicated to how to deal with stress, how to become millionaires and how to find your purpose in life.

Books are important and necessary because they expose people to thoughts. However, it's important not to replicate the thinking process of others. The philosophies of others must serve as a catalyst for developing an individual intellectual platform for understanding the world. Balancing becomes the focus of Montaigne's doctrine. It becomes the fine interrelationship between reason and skepticism. Assuming, for example, that man can rationally prove the existence of God is incorrect; therefore, he must also rely on faith. What is essential is not to arrive at a conclusion, but to continue the discussion for seeking truth. The search and the dialogue must be a continuous wheel in motion. Another definition of skepticism is "fideism," which basically means that someone cannot rely on reason to define religious dogma. It's essential to rely on spiritual revelation and faith.

When Rafael returned to consciousness, it took him a few minutes to realize where he was and what had happened. His front wheel from his black Trek Madone bicycle had slid as he made a 90 degree turn at the intersection of Sweet Home and Old Settler's Way. The lady who had driven up to the stop sign looked at him and asked, "Are you alright?" Rafael responded, "Yes, I think so." He was in a state of shock as the EMS medics stared into his eyes and stated that they were taking him to the nearest emergency room. At first, Rafael informed the medics that he felt good enough to continue his ride. But after seeing a photo of his face taken from his smartphone, he decided it was best to follow their instructions. After speaking to his wife Josefina by phone and explaining what had happened, she encouraged him to go with the medics.

This was an opportune time for Rafael to reflect on the meaning of life. Why did this happen to him? What is the lesson he should learn from this experience? Now, he was forced to deal with an injury on a personal level. God was not to blame for his misfortune. It was a random sequence of elements coming together: a car coming up to a stop sign, fine gravel blending in with the asphalt and a 90 degree turn on a bicycle. The first thought that came to Rafael's mind was: "Why didn't I see the gravel?" He rode over gravel all the time, but there is a difference between riding over gravel in a straight line and turning into it. The distraction of the car approaching the stop sign kept him from thinking about gravel on a turn he normally cut through on a straighter line. It was a time to search for the balance within the act of losing it.

Last night Rafael took his father Nizael to a Spurs basketball game at the AT&T Center in San Antonio, Texas. His father would turn 88 years old in two days on March fourth. Rafael remembered going to many basketball games in Puerto Rico where he grew up. Nizael worked for the Associated Press, so they were able to sit courtside when attending the events. It was fun to see the games played at the speed viewed from that proximity to the court. His father was a good man, but Rafael felt the melancholy of watching his father age. Their conversations were limited to short questions and answers. Rafael would ask, "The Spurs aren't rebounding very well, are they?" Nizael responded, "No, they are not." Rafael would add, "That was fun going to the games in Puerto Rico. His father answered, "I would have preferred to stay there, but your mother wanted to come to Texas." Rafael, now, knew what it was like to watch his dad and mom grow older. He loved them dearly although it was difficult to witness his father lose his mental acumen due to the early onset of Alzheimer's disease.

VIRTUOUS LIVING

THERE IS ANOTHER lesson to learn as a person individually ages and watches his parents grow older. Rafael would often pray: "Dear Lord, give me the presence of mind to love and be there for them as they age. Give me a happy disposition in accepting this along with the compassion and grace that only comes from you." Marcus Aurelius, a Roman emperor born in 121 CE who wrote *Meditations*, came to mind as Rafael thought about stoicism and its meaning in distinguishing between good and evil and how man can control his happiness by understanding the difference between them. Stoicism teaches man that virtue is the only good for himself, and vice is the only evil. In addition, everything else is indifferent regarding his happiness. Therefore, virtue leads to happiness and vice to unhappiness. Marcus believed that the cosmos is a city, and all rational beings are fellow citizens of this metropolis.

If Rafael understood Aurelius correctly, the Roman emperor wanted all citizens to live virtuous lives by respecting the law and by allowing justice to reign in the kingdom among the populace as well as among everyone. If vice were to take hold of man in the form of alcoholism, infidelity and corruption among government officials lusting for power, this would affect the balance of the cosmos. An unbalanced life contradicts the virtuous existence Aurelius suggests for his people. More importantly, according to Rafael, each person must explore the definition of a virtuous life for himself. Marcus Aurelius realized the importance of philosophy by allowing himself to ponder these important questions.

Philosophical inquiries are complex and obtuse because there are no clear-cut answers to these questions. Living a virtuous life for one person is completely different from another's perspective. Virtue for one person may mean living a healthy life whereas for someone else it may entail learning to live gracefully in poverty with a serious health condition. It may involve an individual living peacefully and happily in the direst of circumstances. It may represent an individual adapting to painting portraits with his mouth because he can no longer use his extremities due to paralysis. The human condition is complex and diverse; as a result, the definition of virtue changes.

Why is it of utmost significance to ask these questions and view the answers from a wide and multifarious spectrum? How does man contemplate the greatest good not just for himself but for all citizens of the world? Vice affects each person because it is natural for man to separate himself from the cosmos with his own blinders and boundaries nourished by selfishness and egotism. Philosophy helps him to dialogue and discuss these preoccupations that influence him as a rational being. It is the philosopher who seeks to learn and ask questions. Socrates really understood human nature. Most people will not initiate a conversation with a stranger, whether it be in a church setting or a sporting event, for example. Individuals tend to guard themselves from others. But once the initial question is asked, the conversation flows naturally. Rafael thought it was interesting to notice how neighbors often do not look up to greet him or others when they are passing by on foot or in a car. Where does this human tendency to hide and separate oneself from others come from?

This human characteristic is developed from the time of birth. Children for the most part are taught by their parents to not talk to strangers. This is also endorsed in schools as children move from one grade level to the next. As the world becomes smaller due to the internet and aviation that connect a person instantaneously to someone else, people become more isolated. It takes effort to reach out to another person, and many find themselves with their hands tied by apprehension of others and possibly fear of rejection. This fear drives individuals to hide within the confines of their activities and self-interests. At a recent 5K run that Rafael participated in this past weekend in San Marcos, Texas, he reminisced about a conversation he had with a man who happened to be standing by the water and food table for finishers after the race. They looked at each other, and Rafael asked: "So, for how many years have y'all been having this race?" The man responded: "It's been about eight years now." As they continued their verbal exchange, Rafael learned that the money raised from the race-entry fees was used to buy special lunches for kids in Hays County who were attending school hungry. He stated that Hays County was one of the poorest counties in Texas, and many families could not afford to feed their children properly. Again, the discourse would have never transpired if it were not for the initiative of one person asking the first question.

LOCKE AND AMERICAN POLITICS

IN A WORLD and society dominated by rationality, people tend to show an interest in others and the world around them. Unfortunately, schools and universities teach their pupils, who become part of society, to listen and absorb information but not to question and challenge that knowledge. John Locke, the English philosopher from the seventeenth century, pursued and defended the separation of church and state. The Reformation Period, a movement within Western Christianity of Europe during the sixteenth century that challenged the control and authority of the Roman Catholic Church, was a time when debates existed between Catholics, Protestants, Unitarians, Quakers, atheists and many other religious sects. People could no longer be forced to believe a certain way. Some faiths opposed the Trinity, which acknowledges the Father, Son and Holy Spirit, whereas others believed in the Father as the only figurehead representing the true religion. Rafael remembered having a discussion more than thirty years ago with Umberto, a good friend of his who became a Capuchin priest, who earnestly believed the pope was representative of God and Jesus Christ on earth. Thus, he affirmed that Catholics must revere the pope as God on earth. Rafael disagreed believing that there is only one God in Christ that everyone has the freedom to communicate individually with through prayer.

Locke wrote, "For every church believes itself to be the true church, and there is no judge but God who can determine which of these claims is correct." Again, thinkers like Locke challenged the political and religious authorities of the time that wanted to control and dominate the liberties and freedom of thought of the masses. Therefore, Rafael wanted to express his thoughts on paper to continue this dialogue, one that each individual should have with himself. As he and his wife discussed the current political climate in the U.S. during the early months of 2020, he viewed the ineptness of both the Democratic and Republican Parties. Joe Biden and Bernie Sanders were the prominent Democratic presidential contenders after the recent Super Tuesday voting polls raised them to the favored ones in a previous field of five. One of them would confront Donald Trump during the presidential contest in November.

It is evident in the United States that candidates with the most clout and money are elevated as the upper echelons of contenders interest groups like the medical and oil companies that support them. Rafael inferred that a third political party, one independent from the Democratic and Republican Parties, must emerge in the U.S. This third party must deviate from politics as usual by representing all ethnic groups (Whites, Blacks, Hispanics, Native Americans, Asians and others) with the goal of curtailing the divide created by racism. Both the Democratic and Republican Parties are controlled by the elitists, those who have the most money and power. To establish an even playing field there must be a strong Independent Party that challenges, for example, the simple debate of whether a wall should be built or not along the Mexican and U.S. border. Or, should children and parents of illegal immigrant families be separated or not? The immigration problem is so much more complex than the focus centered on the wall and detention centers.

A presidential candidate, in this case, who speaks English and Spanish fluently is essential. It's extremely important for this candidate to also understand and comprehend the history of Mexican, Central and Latin American history. Why? The U.S. presidential candidate must be able to dialogue with López Obrador, the current Mexican president, in Spanish, his native language, to pressure him to institute more anti-corruption commissions to oversee and retool the political, government, and security agencies that are riddled with corruption and lawlessness that fuel an uneducated society dominated by the drug cartels and poverty. It's a society that benefits only the Mexican elites. The Iran-Contra Affair in the 1980s where Ronald Reagan and his administration assisted the Contra guerrilla troops in their fight against the Somoza regime in Nicaragua only helped slaughter innocent civilians and help prop up a leftist and dictatorial government controlled today by the corrupt and oppressive leadership of Daniel Ortega. Ortega was supposedly a Contra leader in the fight against the Somoza dictator who ruled over Nicaragua for decades. All this instability in Nicaragua and other countries in Central America created fertile ground for the development of gangs and criminal activity. The crime and instability of present-day El Salvador, Guatemala, Honduras and Mexico force families to leave their countries for a better life in the U.S. where the rule of law is enforced.

The U.S. political system lacks balance in dealing with countries like Mexico and Central America in regard to the immigration crisis at the border. The ineptness of Ivy League universities in the U.S. is evident. Most professors in these institutions lean to the Left, meaning they are Democratic in their views of the world. Their history and political departments focus more on American imperialism, which forced itself on countries like Puerto Rico, Cuba and the Philippines during the Spanish American War of 1898 and took the authoritative control of these countries away from Spanish rule. The invasion of the Bay of Pigs in the 1950s by the U.S. Marines in Cuba is another U.S. imperialistic footprint that led to the rule of Fidel Castro and Cuban socialism in 1959. The aim of the leftist academia is to blame the U.S. but not to confront and decry the oppression of the numerous dictators of the Hispanic world like Porfirio Díaz in Mexico, Rafael Trujillo in the Dominican Republic, Hugo Chávez in Venezuela, the Somozas in Nicaragua, Papa Doc in Haiti, Juan Perón in Argentina and many others.

The political balanced perspective can only be established by creating a public spectrum that takes into consideration both sides of an issue like immigration. To do this effectively a candidate must be fluent in both English and Spanish so that he can dialogue effectively with leaders of the Hispanic world. This has never happened in the history of the U.S., but it is the only way to truly ameliorate the crisis at the border. The current political leaders will continue to dismiss this strategy as they continue to focus on whether to build the wall or not. As the American people approach the next presidential election in November of this year, the U.S. again will decide between two older White males, Joe Biden or Donald Trump. The two predominant political parties are incapable of diversifying at this point.

Politics is still dominated by the special interest groups, like the petroleum industry, which are able to spend the most money on their chosen candidates.

BALDWIN AND RACE

JAMES BALDWIN, THE twentieth century Black-American writer, wanted to expose his White audience to the indifference they feel towards Blacks. Baldwin was concerned about presenting the humanity among Blacks and their search for identity as singular individuals. Today, it was evident to Rafael, that Whites and Blacks are still segregated in their cultural environments. In sports, we observe how Black and White athletes compete together with each other along with other ethnic groups, whether they are Hispanic, Asian or European. This is a great experiment in which sports exemplify diversity. However, in other areas of society, such as in government, police departments, schools and neighborhoods, the fences of segregation continue to delineate the separation between races.

Baldwin stated in *Letter from a Region in my Mind* (1962): "Whatever goes up must come down." He went on to affirm: "If we—and now I mean the relatively conscious [W]hites and the relatively conscious [B]lacks, who must, like lovers, insist on, or create, the consciousness of the others—do not falter in our duty now, we may be able, handful that we are, to end the racial nightmare, and achieve our country, and change the history of the world. If we do not now dare everything, the fulfillment of that prophecy, re-created from the Bible in song by a slave, is upon us: *God gave Noah the rainbow sign, no more water, the fire next time!*" Rafael agreed with Baldwin that Blacks and Whites must be of *compos mentis* with each other. If you consider the rhetoric of Malcolm X, a follower of Islam, who claimed that Christ was Black and the White man was the devil, the counter discussion by White Christians that Blacks were descendants of Ham (the youngest son of Noah), who sodomized, castrated, or simply was stunned by Noah's nakedness, according to some biblical scholars. These academic savants also suggest the possibility of the incestuous nature of the relationship between Noah, drunk on wine from his newly planted vineyard, and Ham. As a result, some in "intellectual circles" claim the offspring of Ham were doomed to become slaves because they were not considered to be humans. Whites must put themselves in the place of the Black slaves who were shackled on the European slave ships in Africa and brought over to America. Black slaves in America where treated as objects to be purchased, abused and oppressed by their White masters. You must also remember Blacks enslaved Blacks in Africa in a commercial enterprise that began before arriving to America.

Blacks must also understand that many Whites were brainwashed by their families, churches, schools and governmental institutions to believe their god was White, and they were privileged. History has witnessed this truth from the time of the Inquisition in the fourteenth century in Europe where Christians murdered people of other religious backgrounds if they did not convert to Christianity. This disease spread to other nations ever since 1492 when Columbus and the rest of Europe discovered America and conquered the land owned by the Indigenous people in the name of Christianity. Then, the slave trade from Africa allowed the White man to force Black slaves to work the land. Rafael believed everyone carries this burden and sin, whether he is White, Black or of any other ethnic background because he is human. The White slave owner, who whipped his Black slave, was essentially flogging himself. The Black man, who cannot see himself mirrored in the White slave owner, does not understand the plight of the human condition that is weakened and sickened by power.

Baldwin moved to Paris to remove himself from the racial tensions he experienced in Harlem and the rest of the U.S. in 1948. This allowed him to reflect from a distance on the racial cauldron of hatred brewing in America after World War II. Rafael surmised that this period gave Baldwin time to grow as he learned about Africa from those descendants who lived in France and Europe. Baldwin was also able to grasp a clearer understanding of the plight of the Jews and the European citizens on the other side of the ocean who fought against the Nazi Regime. Paris was a melting pot where intellectuals could freely write and discuss issues pertaining to race and politics. Rafael and his wife knew that travelling to Europe and other countries frees the mind from the traps and blinders that cultures and societies inadvertently impose on their citizens. A person learns to become conscious of other realities that extend beyond his own personal language and barrier.

EXISTENTIALISM AND THE PANDEMIC

RAFAEL COULD SEE how the existentialism espoused by Jean-Paul Sartre, one of the most influential twentieth century philosophers of the Western World, evolved. Sartre affirmed that all people experience anguish because of the freedom man, as a mortal, experiences. Existentialism for him meant that by existing and acting a certain way an individual cohered meaning meaning to his life. He believed there was no fixed design for how someone should be and no god to give him a motive for living. According to Sartre, "[The] lack of pre-defined purpose along with an 'absurd' existence that presents to us infinite choices is what Sartre attributes to the 'anguish of freedom.'"

Sartre spent nine months as a German prisoner of war in 1940, and it was during this time when the seeds of existentialism began to ferment and crystallize in his mind. It seems natural to question the existence of God and the meaning of life. War and incarceration would give him the latitude to reflect on the indoctrination of Nazism and the evil it spread. Much like the Church, during the Inquisition in the fourteenth and fifteenth centuries in Europe that tortured and exterminated those who were not followers of the Church, it would not be uncommon for a person to question the corporeality of the superior being. Sartre's existentialism forces man to not rely on institutions, such as government and churches, to define his destiny and beliefs. He went against the "grain" of the status quo much like Baldwin did in questioning thought patterns that had shaped each individual's view of himself and the world; thus, these stripped him of the freedom to choose and think for himself. Writers compose essays, plays, poems and philosophies to incite people to think outside their box and beyond what the masses mindlessly absorb. When values are inherited without thought, this breeds racism and fanaticism.

It is much easier to accept the views of society in general instead of a fellowman cogitating for himself, which requires great effort and commitment. Again, the art of balancing forces him to view the good and bad of every belief and culture in order to become conscious of the *ethical* and evil coexisting within himself. He must realize the significance of this self-reflection to develop the tools to address the issues that afflict humanity. To not do so is like amputating a hand from his body, which is like removing himself from the injustices imposed on others, because it doesn't affect him individually in the present moment. This is the "essence" Sartre refers to before man becomes aware of the subsistence of his *psyche*. As a child he lives in a state of being, but as he matures he realizes his subjectivity and individuality distinguish him from others. He also realizes he evolves physically, emotionally and spiritually unlike a rock that remains still and does not become cognizant of itself.

Rafael and Josefina pondered the current coronavirus pandemic as they quarantined themselves at home like many others across the nation and rest of the world. Many cruise lines were kept at bay in the sea and not allowed to dock at ports. Yesterday, Rafael woke up feeling a little achy and realized he had a slight fever of 99° that increased to 101°. This morning his temperature went down to 100.1, so this was good because it was decreasing. The hardest part was not being able to exercise yesterday, and he had difficulty sleeping because he had been laying down passively, disjointedly and unwillingly all day. Luckily, Rafael felt much better today. Never in their lifetime had they experienced a pandemic of this nature with thousands of people dying around the world. Schools, restaurants and businesses were closed around the nation. Many small enterprises were shattered economically and closed nationally along with wage earners that could not "survive" the economic recession that was about to ensue. Airports were eerily forced into a standstill, and flights were reduced to a minimum as the world dealt with this pandemic that was overwhelming the healthcare system and affecting the economy negatively. There was a paucity of test kits to check for the coronavirus, and the scientific and medical communities were scrambling to create a vaccine to combat this virus.

During this existential threat created by the virus, Rafael read more about Karl Jaspers' philosophy in the thesis *"Karl Jaspers' Conceptions of the Meaning of Life"* by Kurt Salamun, where he contemplated some of Jaspers' ideas. Jaspers believed existentialism was derived not from the self-rationalization of the individual but from the "gift from Transcendence or God." He further extrapolated that this dimension of being was unknowable. Jaspers didn't view religions in atheistic terms, but he took a critical position against any spiritual conception that seemed to provide objective, guaranteed proofs of the existence of God or was bound to rituals by churches, priests or theologians who pretended to be interpreters of God's will or revelation. Rafael agreed that it was essential to realize that organized religions must encourage its members to search for God subjectively. Many church members turn to the pope, priests and pastors for having the complete proof and knowledge of God to be presented and dispensed to its flock. The leaders have studied the word of God; in many cases, they are experts in understanding God's word. However, they must remember to encourage their affiliates to seek God personally and as a community.

The ritual performed in the Catholic Church of offering the Eucharist at every mass seemed redundant to Rafael, but he understood it was relevant to many Catholics. In evangelical churches, pastors believe members must be saved through baptism showing that now they have accepted Jesus in their lives as Lord and Savior. For many Eastern religions, it is imperative to practice and learn how to meditate quietly, clearing one's mind of the distractions of life, to hear the voice of Buddha or God. Diverse religions and cultures are necessary for our global community to live in peace and harmony. But harm comes from those fanatical and totalitarian perspectives from believers who think their way of worshipping and viewing the world are the only truth. This type of thinking is detrimental to the democracy and peace that must exist between all cultures and people of the world.

From this viewpoint, Rafael and Josefina adhered to the significance of philosophy, which allows a person to learn how to dialogue and respect mindsets differing from his own. This conversation forges a milieu of balance when discussing views of the world. Rafael never believed that this type of discourse could ever take place in the Catholic Church. The rituals of the priest dressing in gowns, preaching behind a pulpit, interpreting the scriptures and preparing the Eucharist seemed totalitarian just as the traditions of other evangelical churches that stressed the narrow concept of "salvation."

WAVES OF THE SAME SEA

IT WAS A sun-drenched day as Rafael ruminated on other topics and pedaled in isolation along rural roads near the outskirts of Seguin on his Speed Madone Trek road bike. In the near distance he saw a man walking his black dog without a leash. As he approached him, the dog darted towards him at full throttle, and the owner's futile words, "Come here," were of no avail. He stopped his bike facing the dog, which caused the animal to halt at a standstill. He asked the man, "How about a leash?" He replied, "It's 'the country.'" After regaining his normal speed on the bike, he thought to himself, "It's 'our' country."

Thoughts like these flooded his consciousness during this uncertain time caused by the anxiety and fear our nation and world were facing due to the coronavirus pandemic. On a recent visit to the grocery store, he was astonished to see the empty shelves where once there was a plethora of toilet paper, sanitizers, eggs, milk and other essential items. He was amazed imagining the satirical images of hoarders loading these items in their carts with tarps and bungee cords to hold everything down. While watching the nightly news, he was flabbergasted to see the masses of young people congregating on beaches in Florida and other areas ignoring the advice from the medical community of social distancing to prevent the spread of the virus.

Moreover, it seems like this worldwide pandemic would bring people closer together in fighting this rampant disease instead of underscoring the selfishness of human nature that some manifest more than others. Even though the majority of Americans and citizens across the world are maintaining their social distance and working from home in an attempt to fight this virus together, Rafael was also surprised to learn of a "fear epidemic" where many were standing in long lines to purchase guns and ammunition to protect themselves from the contagious enemy.

Instead of taking time to reflect individually and collectively on the purpose and meaning of life during this stressful time, one not experienced before in people's lifetime, a person must dig deeper within himself to piece together a serene sense of tranquility during the relentless rocky waves crashing in on him.

The Roman philosopher Seneca wrote, "We are waves of the same sea, leaves of the same tree and flowers of the same garden." These words were written on packages of protective masks sent from China to Italy. Instead of man hoarding and isolating himself philosophically with guns and selfishness, he should remind himself and others that this is not "the" country, but "our" country; thus, it is not the world but our world. Let the pandemic motivate him to be considerate and responsible towards others as he unites and leashes his dog so he and others can solve this problem together without fear but with a profound sense of community.

Instead of viewing himself as "waves of the same sea," man isolates himself within his culture, family and society. Furthermore, he builds fences around his home and job. He has difficulty saying hello to his neighbors when he is outside working in the yard. It is stressful to take his eyes off his smartphone to greet people he passes during his walks throughout the neighborhood.

Many people are only cordial when ordering food at a restaurant by speaking to a waiter or when calling a doctor's office to speak to a receptionist. They only focus on their goals and individual work, which are essential, but they don't see the significance of reaching out to others.

Many young people have lost the simple social politeness of saying "thanks," or sending a thank-you note when they receive a gift from their grandparents or aunts and uncles. Facebook, Instagram and other social media platforms are cesspools of selfishness, narcissism and self-indulgence. A person tries to take the water out of the wave, and by doing this, he drowns in his own self-righteousness and ego consumption. Many attend college and graduate but have not learned to see the connection between themselves and others. They have not developed their own *raison d'être* for living by feeding their souls, bodies and minds. If people are not the same waves of the sea, they become islands submerged under the ocean and lose the oxygen and fiber that bridges them to themselves and others. They become zombies existing in a selfish nebula of nonexistence within the abyss of nothingness.

Rafael knew that he was no exception to falling into this abyss from time to time. He realized that he needed to refocus on his spiritual life and God on a daily basis. Moments of self-doubt and self-centeredness crept into his consciousness sporadically, especially, now, that he was semiretired and not working much as an interpreter due to the coronavirus pandemic. Rafael continued to run and bike, but the gyms were temporarily closed, so he couldn't swim and lift weights. There was quite a bit of idle time, and as Josefina would reassure him, "An idle mind gives the Devil a foothold." Sometimes, the pressure of taking care of his sister, who was receiving dialysis treatment three times a week, and his elderly parents was a bit overwhelming. He was constantly aware, more so as he aged, of the necessity of sitting quietly, centering and praying. At times, he didn't feel the ongoing peace and tranquility that meditation should provide.

THE POPE AND GANG VIOLENCE IN CENTRAL AMERICA

THE OTHER NIGHT Rafael and Josefina watched the movie *The Two Popes* on Netflix. He thought about Pope Frances, and how he confronted the corruption and gang violence in the Central American Triangle (Guatemala, El Salvador and Honduras). Pope Frances, being from San Lorenzo, Argentina, should be able to understand and communicate the need for change and reforms in those countries. It is more than just visiting those countries and providing them with the Eucharist and admonishing the corrupt government for their practices and exploitations. After reading some about the origins of the gangs in Central America, especially the MS13, Rafael learned many Salvadorians immigrated to Los Angeles during the Salvadorian Civil War in the early 1980s. Many did not fit into the American culture and as a result they were marginalized. They developed a counterculture influenced initially by the music of rock bands like AC/DC and Metallica. Many were uneducated and young; thus, they succumbed to the gang life to form a type of community. They also became affiliated with the Mexican Mafia, which controlled most of the illegal activities within the prison system. The number in the acronym MS-13 references "M," which is the thirteenth letter in the alphabet. This association indicates their loyalty to the Mexican Mafia. The MS means Mara Salvatrucha where Mara stands for gang, Salva refers to being from El Salvador, and trucha translates into street smarts. Many of the immigrants were deported back to El Salvador once the war was over in 1992. As a result, the gangs spread throughout the rural and urban areas of Central America extorting businesses and homeowners in their barrios to pay them monthly rents. The gang members are known for their extreme violence and mutilations with machetes imposed on those who do not consent to their demands. They also recruit young boys and girls to join their gangs, and family members are kidnapped and tortured if they don't abide by their rules.

Understanding the problems of immigrants coming from Central America to the U.S. is a complicated matter that cannot be solved only by building or not building a wall between the Mexican and U.S. border. Unfortunately, the wall dominates the political discussions of most Democrats and Republicans in the United States. Most of the knowledge of Central and South America is acquired from travelling Americans who spend most of their time in beach resorts drinking margaritas and reading John Grisham books as they sit in a lounge chair soaking up the sun. Americans also depend on newspapers and blogs for information on the latest news in those areas of the world. Americans who do settle in these countries in the south usually live in their own *colonias*, separating themselves from the native people of those communities. A prime example is the *gringo* colony of San Miguel de Allende in Mexico where many North Americans have settled and bought homes, and where English is more dominant than Spanish.

THE SOULLESSNESS OF THE CHURCH

THE NEED TO dwell within the confines of a person's cultural enclave is natural philosophically and scientifically because like-minded people speaking the same language with the same social norms are attracted to one another. Isaac Newton, the English mathematician and philosopher from the seventeenth century, discovered the concept of gravitational pull when an object, such as an apple, falls to the ground. It falls in a straight line, not to one side or another. He also applied the concept of gravity to the universe beyond the earth. Philosophically, Newton believed nature and the universe functioned much like a synchronized clock; therefore, there must be a designer or superior being, God, who established this order and consistency. He believed God was ubiquitous and existed in all forms of matter and life. However, René Descartes, the French mathematician and philosopher from the sixteenth century believed that God created the world but existed elsewhere; thus, God was not found in all forms of matter and life. As a result, Descartes thought God could not control certain events that occurred on earth, for example, because He lived elsewhere in a kingdom separate from man. Newton's gravitational equation demonstrates the relationship between gravity, mass and distance between the objects' centers.

$$E_{grav} \propto \frac{m_1 * m_2}{d^2}$$

where E_{grav} represents the force of gravity between two objects

$\propto$ means "proportional to"

m_1 represents the mass of object 1

m_2 represents the mass of object 2

d represents the distance separating the objects' centers

Rafael was interested in the scientists like Newton and Descartes who also applied their empirical knowledge to theology and the understanding of God. Oftentimes, in the school and university curriculums in the U.S. and across the world, professors separate academic subjects from one another. Students learn about math, biology, political science, literature, philosophy, theology and other subjects separately. This is unfortunate because students don't learn that all subjects are interconnected as they can extrapolate from the prototype of the gravitational equation presented by Newton, suggesting that God is the designer of this concept and all scientific and mathematical principles discovered by man. Josefina and Rafael witnessed this separation of knowledge, especially in churches. Priests from the Catholic Church along with pastors from Baptist, Episcopalian, Methodist and other denominations were at fault. Many church leaders wonder why their members are leaving the Church. In Rafael's mind the main reason is because services, especially sermons, are extremely boring and repetitive.

Jesus would want churches to focus on the Eucharist, but Rafael was sure Christ would want churches to be invigorating and stimulating. Imagine a sermon in which a priest presents an apple and allows it to fall into a bucket of water as he references the gospel. Spiritually, humans feel a gravitational pull towards God. Sermons and homilies today should be interjected with illustrations like these from the sixteenth century and other periods to enhance the meaning of God's word. Theology becomes stagnant when the Gospels are only delivered in a noncritical manner, repeating the miracles of Jesus feeding thousands with a few fish and a couple of loaves of bread, Christ walking on the sea, God telling us to love our neighbors, care for the poor and follow the ten commandments. These are all very important lessons that should be taught and reiterated often. But how do the biblical stories relate to history and philosophy? Why not include a different philosopher into the sermon each month and relate it the theological message?

Blaise Pascal, the French scientist and theological philosopher from the seventeenth century, studied probabilities, the vacuum of pressures and invented the syringe. Towards the end of his life, he became more interested in religious matters and believed God could not be proved by reason. A follower could only know God by his divine grace and a person's faith in Christ. He wrote *Pensées* in which he developed his ideas pertaining to religion. He emphasized it was better to believe because if salvation were true, man would enjoy the blessings of living with God in Heaven. Even if he did not truly believe in God, it was better to trust in God because why should he take a chance in there not being a Heaven if there really was one. In other words, it's better to take a chance in believing because there is nothing to lose. If someone does not confess his allegiance to God, he could risk spending eternity in Hell. So, it's best to have faith in God because if there is a Heaven, man gains everything; if there is no such place, he loses nothing.

These types of divagations would help the Church to gain more popularity and greater attendance allowing its community of followers to grow. The same sermons grow stagnant and monotonous week after week and year after year. Priests and pastors have the academic background to explore and relate biblical truths to history, the arts and philosophy, but many choose not to do so. The Eucharist becomes meaningless unless churches find ways to break from tradition. Carmen, a wonderful lady who cleans Rafael and Josefina's home every two weeks, stated in their regular *wiri wiri* (slang for irrelevant mini-dialogues) that in many Catholic Churches the congregation is primarily a conglomerate of older members, and they are not interested in hearing homilies interspersed with references to Aristotle, Plato, Descartes, da Vinci and other thinkers. They prefer the plain-Jane version of theology, and this is another exemplification of why young people are leaving the Church. Theology should be bold, enriching and stimulating and not dull, monotonous and boring.

THE TOXICITY OF THE PANDEMIC WITHIN ACADEMIA

THE CORONAVIRUS HAS wreaked havoc in our nation as the death toll reached 10,000 in New York City. It is a virus that knows no border as thousands of deaths are recorded across the globe reaching every corner of the world. The U.S. healthcare systems are overwhelmed by a lack of face masks, quicker testing measures, ventilators, beds and a sufficient amount of nurses and doctors to care for the sick. It is recorded in Chicago that a disproportionate number of Black Americans will die from the virus because many of them don't have equal access to medical care due to poverty and the fact that many of them earn minimum wages; therefore, they are unable to stay home and work from their computers. Many are bus drivers, cooks in restaurants and sanitation workers, for example. It's extremely sad the poorest citizens are the most vulnerable to being infected by the virus. Yes, in many cases, this is a reflection of the lack of opportunities for many, but it's also a reality that many African Americans prefer to isolate themselves within their communities without branching out and seeking contingency plans to educate themselves through grants and other governmental aid to help them realize their dreams. This attitude is not exclusive of just the African-American culture, but it is also prevalent among poor Whites, Hispanics and other ethnic groups that exist in the U.S. It's a "cultural pandemic" that expands and infects the minds of many across our nation and the world.

Rafael learned, as he shifted through the world of academia, that politics, unfortunately, affects every stage of learning and the working world. He found this out quickly when he attended graduate school at the University of Texas in the late 1980s in Austin. Professors in the Department of Spanish and Portuguese made it clear to their students this was an institution that stressed inquiry, research and publications by its professors.

Learning was a secondary by-product of the colossal academic machine functioning as a *bulldozer* for anything getting in its way of investigations for the sake of gaining a worldwide reputation for leading the way, establishing itself as a top-notch university and part of the "Ivy League system." This type of approach creates an imbalance between learning and research. Research and academic inquiries are indispensable but not at the expense and negligence of *quality pedagogical cultivation*. "Scholarly professors" should prioritize educating so that their deserving intelligent *tutees* become successful catechumens of the knowledge dispensed to them. Since this approach is not the norm, academia is full of libraries with journals covered in dust and cobwebs that nobody reads, except for the .001 percent that do "noncritical cogitative" research. Rafael soon realized professors were competing against each other, and they had their "favorite students" who agreed with their political and intellectual points of view. This was a precedent of "liberal Biden and Obama political-favoritism and racism" against Christians and non-Christians, specifically all African Americans, Hispanics, Asians and all minorities in the United States and abroad; especially, all poor, middle class and affluent Caucasians, regardless of their religious beliefs, that Rafael witnessed firsthand.

Later, as Rafael began to teach, he was exposed to the politics of the administration at the high school and community college levels. In high school the school board, superintendent, principals, vice principals and parents usually formed a tight bond with the teachers on the other side of the fence playing the political game of appeasing to their demands. Unruly and undisciplined students were often returned to the classroom, and teachers were blamed for not having a proficient behavioral plan in place to control and create a learning environment. Parents were quick to blame teachers and the administration for the failures their children experienced in the classroom. Parents and administrators were satisfied with teachers who adjusted grades so that all students passed, whether they deserved to or not. Rafael became cognizant of the need to save and invest as much money as possible to be in a position someday of not being subjected to the politics of the academic and working world. This became one of his priorities.

At the community college level, the schism between full-time professors and adjunct instructors was the norm. Full-time professors were tenured for life, and many stayed employed well beyond retirement age. Rafael worked as an adjunct instructor for many years teaching Spanish at Texas State University, Trinity University, Austin Community College, San Antonio College and Texas Lutheran College from the 1990s through the 2000s. Penetrating this divide was an impossible feat because the system was entrenched in separating the hierarchy of the full-timers from the part-timers. Even though many adjunct instructors were by far better teachers, it was a barrier that could not be surpassed. Again, Rafael learned earnestly the necessity to save and earn enough money to create his own opportunities regardless of the *politicos'* agenda. Otherwise, a person is enslaved by the institutions that form part of society.

FINANCIAL FREEDOM AND DICKINSON'S POETRY

EVERY CLASS AND race in America are subject to the politics established by capitalism or any other type of government. The beauty of a democracy like the one in the U.S. is that a person, as an individual and citizen, can make choices, and he truly has the freedom to save or not to save money to forge opportunities for himself. Rafael learned another valuable lesson twenty years ago after a difficult divorce. Luckily, everything was handled legally, but Rafael was stuck with paying the mortgage for a house worth $260,000 on five acres. He couldn't afford it on a teaching salary as an adjunct instructor at Texas State University and Austin Community College. In addition, Rafael was paying off many returned checks for insufficient funds since the whole fiasco caused him to overlook some of his other financial obligations. It was an extremely stressful time in his life, one that he promised not to relive. He had also started working the night shift at Super Stop, a convenient store, where he could get food and have it credited to him before being deducted from his paycheck. Rafael slept an average of three to four hours a night on a rollout mat in the living room downstairs of their two-story home where it was much cooler since he did not run the air conditioner to save money. He also commuted between Austin and San Marcos, Texas while teaching at the different college campuses. Oftentimes, he would stop on a side road on the way between the two cities to take a nap under the shade of a large canopied oak tree. Luckily, he hired a good lawyer who had him tabulate all his assets as she did with hers, and everything ended up being divided equally between the two of them.

After several months of litigation, the divorce was finalized, and Rafael received half of the equities pertaining to their investments with Edward Jones. He also received full ownership of the home, which fortunately, he was able to sell for $230,000. He vowed to be debt free once everything settled. He paid off the remaining balance of $20,000 on his mortgage, and he bought a home in Canyon Lake for $73,000 in cash. The promissory note on his Toyota truck was also paid off, and the rest of the money was invested in his accounts with Edward Jones. When it was all said and done, he learned a valuable lesson about finances. He vowed to remain debt free for the rest of his life. His prayers were answered as he totally relied on God to get him through this distressing period of his life. Upon further reflection he realized he could have lost everything and could have ended up homeless. Not having children made things easier from a legal and financial standpoint.

If a person saved and invested some money every month, he would eventually reach a point in his life where he could make his own choices pertaining to employment and retirement. Working for someone else and playing the "political game" was one he didn't want to do for the rest of his life. The freedom to start an individual's own business or pursue his hobby was the only way to go. However, the majority of Americans live from paycheck to paycheck and spend well above their means. It's easy to lose a sense of financial steadiness when someone, as it is the case for many Americans, is bombarded constantly by advertising, suggesting and reminding him of all the new things and gadgets he needs to buy and "materialistically devour."

As the coronavirus raged on, Rafael thought of Emily Dickinson, the American poet, who was born in 1830 in Amherst, Massachusetts and died in the same city in 1886. She attended the Mount Holyoke

Female Seminary in South Hadley for one year and then returned home. Not only did Dickinson become homesick, but she did not return to her seminary studies because she did not believe in Christ the way the institution wanted her to believe in Him. She still had many questions about her faith, and she needed time to reflect on her religious inquiries and answers. Emily loved her father and sister who lived with her. Her brother married and lived next door. She spent all of her adult life living at home and writing poetry in her room on the second floor. There is no doubt she led a reclusive and monastic life.

Dickinson rebelled against the Calvinistic Church and its strict dogma. She didn't believe it was necessary to go to church to hear God's message, and it wasn't necessary to make a public proclamation of her faith to the rest of the world. Her letter writing and poems were the means by which she could learn about God and come to know Him. She writes, "Because I could not stop for Death, He kindly stopped for me… The carriage held but just ourselves and immortality." It was interesting Dickinson spent most of her time inside a home writing poetry. She dedicated her life contemplating her spirituality and humaneness and preferred the company of her thoughts. Most of her intellectual conversations involved speaking to her younger sister Lavinia, her brother Austin and her father. She read voraciously and admired the poetry of Emerson and Thoreau, but she did not classify herself as a transcendentalist. Dickinson was only true to herself, and she was not a leader or a follower. Perhaps the fact that she was simply herself made her transcendental.

After watching the film, *The Quiet Passion,* which was about Emily Dickinson's life, Josefina and Rafael thought it was interesting to learn of a woman who held such a high standard for herself. She never married even though she fell in love with a gifted orator and priest who was married. He showed an interest in her poetry, which was unusual for the time because women then weren't expected to participate in the arts. This was a vocation and domain for men only. Her love was short lived because he was married, and she never expressed her feelings towards him. Furthermore, she was a prolific letter writer who communicated with her friends and acquaintances through this medium. Many times, she would include a poem she had written in her letters.

Dickinson explores the life of a poet by stating: "This was a Poet—it is That…Distills amazing sense…From ordinary meanings—And Attar so immense… The Poet--it is He—Entitles us—by Contrast—to ceaseless Poverty." She had the luxury of not worrying about making a living since her father was a lawyer, and they were well-to-do. Being of privilege Dickinson could devote her time to writing poetry because for her it was more about living her passion and examining her life. She refused to live her life tied to the domestic responsibilities of cleaning, cooking and taking care of a home. By exposing herself to knowledge through reading, she freed herself to design and explore her inner world.

There is much a person can learn from musing over the writings of Emily Dickinson, an American woman and writer, who became the voice of American literature. She was a woman not influenced by the intellectual movement of the nineteenth century in which a woman was destined to a life bound by marriage and taking care of the household. She did not seek fame as a scholar and only became known as a poet after her death. Her only intention was to define herself in a world where women did not have a voice. As Rafael contemplated Dickinson's life, he could she how many today in the twenty-first century were controlled by technology, work and activities that take them away from true reflection. Everyone needs time to think and write within the boundaries of his solitude to commune with God because his spirit cries out for him to do so. Dickinson listened to her calling, and she pursued it with an unapologetic passion.

TITANIUM PLATES AND IMPRESSIONISM

IT WAS FIVE in the morning on December 6, 2019 when Rafael's alarm clock awoke him and Josefina from a deep sleep. They hesitantly slid out of bed as they prepared themselves to go to Brooks Army Medical Center for a 7:00 a.m. appointment for Rafael's surgery to insert two titanium plates into the left side of his face. The surgeons would repair two small bones in his left cheek in the zygotic area. Rafael shivered and was unnerved with the thought of the surgeon's scalpel slicing about a two-inch incision on the inside of his upper lip. The surgeon believed it was necessary to repair these bones so they could heal properly. Otherwise, there could be a noticeable depression in his face, and the other bone could potential affect his sinuses if it was not placed in a plate to heal correctly.

Josefina's presence was comforting to Rafael as he slipped into his surgery gown and grey socks. A nurse anesthetist came in soon after to insert an IV in his right hand. Shortly afterwards, Dr. Zane came in to his cubicle to discuss the procedure with him and Josefina. He wore a beanie with images of bicycles on it in order to ease the anxiety of the moment for Rafael. A small incision would be made on the outside of the cheekbone to pull on that area for the plates to be inserted correctly. Rafael and Josefina liked Dr. Zane, and they were confident the procedure would be successful. The anesthesia was administered as Rafael held Josefina's hand and said, "I love you, Baby." His bed was wheeled away to the surgery room, and he was lifted on to another bed. He saw the lights overhead as he drifted asleep.

Rafael's thoughts turned to the water lilies painted by Oscar-Claude Monet, the famous French impressionist artist of the nineteenth century. It's intriguing to note Monet became frustrated with the *Académie*, France's "exclusive" art establishment, because it only accepted formulaic works of the ancient Greek and Roman myths displayed in the Louvre. Monet had a passion for painting outdoors and for creating his own work. In his late 20s, he was broke financially, depressed and attempted suicide by jumping off a bridge into the Seine River. He survived his suicide attempt and began to spend time with other artists who rejected the *Académie's* restrictions. He became friends with Pierre-Auguste Renoir, Camille Pissarro, Edgar Degas and Paul Cézanne. Renoir spent time with Monet in the summer of 1873 in a home Monet was renting in Argenteuil, a suburb of Paris. There Renoir painted *Monet Painting at His Garden in Argenteuil*.

There is no doubt Monet suffered a spiritual crisis when he attempted suicide. Here was a young artist trying to find his way by defying the societal conventions of the time. He did not want to be like most artists who mimicked the art of the classical world in order to make a living. The friendships he established with Renoir, Pissarro, Degas and Cézanne avowed him to find his own path and to flourish as an artist in his own right. The group called themselves, The Anonymous Society of Painters, Sculptors, Printmakers, etc. They presented an exhibit in 1874, which included artwork with thick and spontaneous brush strokes with vivid and bright colors. A critic compared Monet's work *Impression, Sunrise* to an unfinished sketch, and the term "Impressionist" evolved to depict this new art form.

Rafael was fascinated by the term "unfinished" because it reflected and depicted life in its most elemental stage. Just like "balancing" everyone attempts to maintain an equilibrium within the ups and downs of life. There was a quote he remembered from a Nike commercial, which stated, "There is no finish line." Artists like Monet would not have evolved if there were no sunrises or lilies to paint. If he could not see and envision the shades of light throughout the day on the natural subjects he painted, he would not have been able to conceive them. His art became his meaning for living and participating in the world. Thousands of viewers and artists globally view Monet's many works displayed across museums worldwide and are mystified by the footprints of *nonfigurative* matrices he left behind. The depictions of paint, brushstrokes, water, lilies and shades of light and verdant colors are sold for millions. The admirers look at his art among many others and exclaim in awe, "Why?"

What is it that draws the artist to paint, the songwriter to sing, the writer to write and the golfer to play golf, for instance? Biologically and physiologically man needs to eat in order to live. Humans also have a mind, heart and soul that must be nourished. Similarly, an uncontemplated life is one lived without the sustenance to give it meaning. Without sun, water and soil, a plant dies and fades away. Without an ingenious outlet, a person loses his "balance" in a world that encourages him to follow the crowd and give up his identity. He becomes consumed, for example, with aging and fearing death. He tries to buy the latest products to reduce the wrinkles on his face. Birth, living and death are the light, colors and water *lilies* of his individual life. The crow's-feet become the bright colors he chooses to paint or hide throughout the process of living. Upon death he will decompose into a carcass of dirt, and he will transform into the fossils that fuel the energy of future generations.

Rafael's "noetic deliberations" shifted back into the past as he tried to recollect the first time he attempted to ride a bicycle without training wheels in Puerto Rico. Pedro, a neighborhood friend with a blue bicycle, let him borrow it and told him to get on it and start pedaling as fast as he could. Rafael abided by strumming the pedals for about four rotations and then falling to his right side tearing a hole in the knee area of his jeans. It did not occur to him at that distant moment that this was the beginning of a lifelong journey and enjoyment of riding a bicycle. Rafael might have thought contrarily if he would have been able to see into the future and predict his new predication at the hand of the surgeon who was about to slice a two-inch opening into the upper part of the inside of his mouth. After the third fall, he mastered and controlled his *stasis* as he gained speed rolling down a hill. Not knowing how to use the brakes properly, he slid onto some lush grass and came to a halt before running into a tree. The sense of freedom and movement on a two-wheeler fueled the *magic* Rafael still experiences today as he rides and races in triathlons on a regular basis.

Suddenly, Rafael's attention veered back to the present and his black bookcase resting in the nook of the corner wall of his study. His eyes were drawn to a group of nine small books of well-known artists: Klimt, Constable, Cézanne, Turner, Renoir, Degas, Manet, Gauguin and Lautrec. He opened Renoir's book and read his brief biography. Auguste Renoir was born in Limoges, France in 1841 and deceased in Cagnes in 1919. He was one of the founders of Impressionism. It is striking to remark that his early works along with those of other emerging artists, like Monet, Sisley and Morisot, were derided by the art establishment of Paris and were not selected to be viewed in the official Salon in the early 1870s. Renoir later enjoyed some success displaying his work in two Impressionistic exhibitions in 1876. His painting of *Madame Charpentier and Her Children* gained recognition when it was finally accepted for viewing in the Salon in the aforementioned year.

In 1881 Renoir visited Italy, and he was impressed with the Italian Renaissance painters. He then decided to *tighten* his line and do away with the Impressionistic method of applying color in small, thin and visible brush strokes, emphasizing the depiction of light as it changes. The traditional way of painting was to apply hues of colorful pigment layered in glazes. Renoir now concentrated on combining what he learned about color from his Impressionistic foray with traditional techniques of administering paint. It was hard not to admire *Bathers in the Seine, La Grenouillère* from 1869. The broken streaks of the thick *liquid medium* he manipulated with brushstrokes to depict the reflections in the water along with the brilliant shadows of light streaking the clothes of the men and women of the day walking along the promenade are refreshing. A sense of stillness is felt by the black and white dog resting at the foot of the canvas as the viewer sees a small white sailboat drifting along. It was something a student would observe in an art class with a desire emanating from within to want to go visit the Seine in France.

CYCLING AND RIGHT THINKING

THIS MORNING RAFAEL met with Ramón, a good friend, he had known now for about 25 years at Cibolo, Texas to do a 52-mile bike ride. It was a bright but crisp 44 degrees with a fairly strong northerly wind. They had both been doing triathlons for approximately 30 years in the Hill Country of Central Texas. It was the off-season, so they would be doing a leisurely ride, which gave them some time to catch up on things. Ramón's doctor reported that he had a high calcium buildup of about 1,200 grams around the exterior of his heart. However, he was not experiencing any shortness of breath or chest pain. The inside of his heart had no calcium or obstruction at all. It was a real mystery because he had completed several Ironman races over the years and was in great shape. An Ironman consists of a 2-mile swim, a 112-mile bike ride and a 26.1 mile run. It takes a lot of training and effort to complete this extreme endurance event. Ramón would often finish this event in anywhere from 14 to 16 hours. They had a great ride, and their thoughts flowed from one topic to the next with each pedal stroke.

Rafael's thoughts returned to the book *The Heart of the Buddha's Teaching* by Thich Nhat Hahn. Hahn discussed the significance of "right thinking" where he disagrees with Descartes who states, "I think, therefore I am." Hahn believes the opposite, "I think, therefore I am not." In the Buddhist tradition, an excess amount of thinking separates the mind from the body; therefore, a person feels more anxiety because his mind never rests. When he breathes deeply and slows his mind down, he is in a better place for experiencing joy, peace and happiness. Hahn emphasizes that there are two parts to thinking—initial thought (*vitarka*) and developing thought (*vichara*). An individual may initially think, "I need to go to the grocery store this afternoon." A developing thought would follow, "I wonder if I have everything I need to purchase on my list."

According to Hahn, in the first stage of meditation concentration (*dhyana*), both kinds of thinking are present. In the second state neither one is there; thus, the mind is empty of thoughts for a moment for clarity to set in. Rafael remembered listening to his father Nizael teach a Sunday school class when he was in middle school in San Juan, Puerto Rico. Rafael thought about God by asking his father, "What does God mean to you?" Nizael asked him the same question: "What does God mean to you?" This allowed Rafael to stay in the moment and listen to his own thoughts instead of adding a new concept to think about. A person begins to realize when he stops the chattering of the mind he is able to rest in the moment and enjoy his "tea." Many times work consumes man's mind with thinking about all the things he needs to do. He must let go of those ruminations in order to remain and dwell in the present. What a challenge it is for him to linger breathing peacefully in the now!

Memories of sitting in the sanctuary of the Union Church every Sunday morning at Punta Las Marías in San Juan, Puerto Rico at 11 am flooded Rafael's mind. The church was located two blocks from the sounding surf of the northeastern waves of the curvaceous coast. There was always a brightness to each day as the cascading dance of palm trees and the *piragüero* waited for beachgoers coming to spend some time by the water. The songs of the choir became monotonous and boring much like the sermons vociferated each week. He already knew the stories about King David, Abraham and Christ. Christ performed many miracles and overturned the tables in the church where merchants were selling their goods. He was crucified by the Jews and Romans and rose on the third day. Christ forgives each person of his sins once he accepts him as savior in his life. Rafael wondered, "Why do you need to be reminded of these stories every Sunday?"

Just like breathing in and out slowly, man needs to practice rightful thinking, speaking and acting according to Nhat Hanh when he discusses the heart of the Buddha. Rafael believed a person searches for God and his meaning through the action of breathing. When he stops the flood of thoughts by breathing, he is in a better position to hear and feel God. When he sits in front of a computer screen with the redness of a poinsettia plant in view, he can see God. God is the tint of redness in each leaf, and He is the lines that are geometrically joined in the seams of the flower and leaf. Water, sun and air are absorbed through the roots of this plant and transported by these vessels throughout its network of lines. Who else could have created such a spectacular and marvelous canvas of vegetation?

Rafael felt connected to the world through his breathing and eyesight:

"Breath of the Wheel"

A bike ride with Ramón zigzagging the country
roads of Cibolo and Seguin with the cold breeze
cutting through our chests,
The conversation flowed from health, races, trips
to be taken to Israel, Greenland, Africa,
Ramón with his black and grey ponytail tucked
under his Catlike helmet,
I felt the roughness of the road beneath me,
Years of riding, training, meditating brought
me to the same place year after year,
Why?
The glory of a medal appeared and disappeared
with each rotation of my tire,
The health benefits to die a late death,
The search for meaning fulfilling the soul
with a quest of a lifetime…

TO WRITE OR NOT TO WRITE

RIGOBERTO, THE HUSBAND of Josefina's friend Bernarda, had stopped by to spend the night at Rafael and Josefina's home. He was on his way back to Hermosa Beach, California from New Orleans. He had long, shoulder-length, grey hair and wore his clear white glasses like a headband. His eyes sparkled with energy, and he stood in the remodeled kitchen with Asics sneakers, faded blue jeans and an oversized sweater. He discussed the previous day and night he spent in Goliad, the historical town of significance to the Alamo and the War of 1836 between the Texians and the Mexican troops led by Santa Anna. Rigoberto only stayed for about twenty minutes before taking off to look at Christmas lights at Incarnate Word University, the Pearl District and downtown San Antonio. He dropped off his night bag in the room upstairs walking up the lightly stained wood steps. Josefina gave him a key so that he could let himself in since they would be asleep when he returned.

Rafael meditated on the things man does as a human being: travel, converse, sleep, eat, exercise and numerous other activities. Why do some people write while others observe with no intention of writing? Why does someone like Renoir paint while others don't? Why do some like Nhat Hanh become monks while others don't? Why does a cardinal with its crested feathers on its head sit on the patio railing basking in the sun with its dark hues of red feathers? These are some of the multitude of questions a person asks himself quietly or out loud. One question Rafael found himself contemplating lately was: "Why do I write? Do I want others to read my books of poetry?" Of course, it's human nature to want others to examine someone's work like those who peruse the books of Dickens, Steinbeck, Homer, Dante, Voltaire, Diderot, Rousseau, Sartre, Descartes, Cervantes, Unamuno, Dickinson, Langston Hughes, Nietzsche, Robert Frost, Walt Whitman, Carl Jung, Socrates, Plato, Borges, Rubén Darío, Gabriela Mistral, Vasconcelos and the plethora of others whose books fill personal libraries. In the universities the great writers of the past and present centuries are studied and researched by students and professors in their liberal arts program. What can you learn from them?

As Rafael awoke from being unconscious after taking that spill on his bicycle this time last year, he asked himself these questions. The art of balancing requires an individual to get back up and to rebalance everything: his priorities, philosophy for living, relationships and soul. Writing is like breathing much like riding a bicycle is about pedaling and maintaining a person's balance. Writing is about expressing and devising an outlet for someone's thoughts; it's not about being published and read by others. Sure, this would be nice, but too much emphasis is placed on marketing a person's work and selling it to others. Many make a living by doing so, but for Rafael there was much more to writing than this. Just like Nhat Hanh encourages man to be kind with his speech to others, an individual also needs to be amiable with himself to reach below the surface of what society expects of him. Rafael knew he needed to be compassionate to himself with his words and his writings. Writing is not about fame but about man knowing himself, a voyage of a lifetime.

Josefina and Rafael lived on a winding street, and there was a residential and commercial painter who lived down the street with his wife. They were in their 60s, which was about the same age as Rafael and Josefina. The painter owned an old turquoise and white pickup truck with a camper top with the insignia *Diggs* on its door panels. They were usually outside taking care of their immaculate yard, and they had been residents of this old San Antonio neighborhood for most of their lives. If he wasn't tinkering in his lawn mowing raking leaves or fixing the sprinkler system, he was working in his garage rearranging paint supplies there and in his vehicle. Every once in a while when Rafael would drive by, he would look to try to catch their attention to greet them with a simple wave. Rarely, did they look up, and on the few times they did, Rafael would wave. The man would wave as if his privacy had been invaded. They didn't appear to be happy even though they consistently did their chores. Rafael wondered, "Do we wake each day with the sole purpose of doing chores and marking them off our list?" It sure seems like this was the case.

Why does the poet or philosopher exist? There has to be a meaning beneath the surface of doing. The modern world has taken man away from who he is. Rafael remembered walking through the quaint streets of Florence, Italy many years ago. It fascinated him to hear the water trickling in the numerous fountains on the streets and watch artists painting with their scaffold, paint and brushes in the silent corners of the city. They stood, observed and painted. It seemed like a surreal moment in which they stopped in the midst of the razzle-dazzle of moving from one place to another, of accomplishing one errand after another and of busying themselves with some sort of activity to observe, record, create and to be. A poet exists to write and discover, not to be read or understood. A philosopher exists to think so as not to influence others but as a means to understand himself. "Do not ask me what I believe?" for that is not the important question. The critical task at hand for the poet and philosopher is to express, conceive and pursue for the sake of defining his beliefs for himself and no one else. In a world in which many strive for fame and approval from others, man must learn to seek in his own solitude the meaning of life for himself and no one else. This is the ultimate duty of the poet, philosopher and artist.

DECONSTRUCTION OF THE BREATH

MANY YEARS AGO while teaching at Austin Community College in Austin, Texas, Rafael thought about some of the students he had more than twenty years ago. Richard was one particular student who stood out for his creativity and class presentations. Every couple of weeks the class was required to prepare and present skits. Richard and his partner dressed up in Batman and Robin outfits with their black and red capes swirling in the air. They talked about their next adventure in a high octane voice in Spanish as they ordered burritos and tacos at Taco Bell. They incorporated vocabulary and grammatical concepts they had been learning in class. Richard was a theater major who was working on writing a script for a movie. He became good friends with Rafael after the semester ended. Eventually, Richard introduced him to the late Joseph Campbell, a well-known professor of comparative religion. In his book *Historical Atlas of World Mythology*, Campbell describes the "OM!" sound of the *Upanishad*. He states, "This perishable sound is all. As further explained: it is the Past, the Present, and the Future, all that has become, is becoming, and is yet to be. Moreover, whatever transcends this three-fold Time: that also is OM."

The outside light was visible to the open shutter in front of the black desk where Rafael was sitting and writing on his computer. A black metallic lamp with a black shade was sustained by the design of the Eiffel Tower. It was a quiet moment in which he enjoyed looking at the shapes from the trees slightly swaying on the asphalt of the street among the panorama of red blossoms from a tree captured through the lens of an opened white-wooden panel. What was this need to reflect on the OM of the *Upanishad*? Why was there an interest in focusing on the past, present and future? There is no doubt a person's mind is flooded with thoughts every single hour of the day, causing distractions and confusion at times. The Buddhist emphasizes the need to focus on the present, and if an individual really vociferates the OM sound, it does have a calming effect on the body and mind. According to Rafael writing and sitting still also serve the same purpose because a person is taking the time to center himself and ponder the meaning of his existence. This is nothing novel or new to mankind, but it is easy for modern man to avoid this calling to find and maintain a balance between his emotional and spiritual being.

Rafael's next breath led him to open a *reticente* book adjacent to him resting on an elongated-corner bookcase in which he was attracted to the beautiful glossy black cover with images of a wicked sea descending on fishermen painted by Joseph Turner (1775-1851), the famous artist born in London. The waves rise from birth and fall into death according to Nhat Hanh. Clarence Jones writes, "Turner's message—that man is unaware and little concerned with his destiny—led his work into the deep waters of metaphysics, with paint becoming a medium, not for depicting scenery but for describing the unseen forces that govern man's destiny." Paint for Turner became the poet's ink for delving within to seek and depict the mysteries and hidden gems he seeks to comprehend. Man's intellectual being strives to rationalize the natural world around him, but the artist deconstructs this urge with his medium.

"Disentangled Water"

<blockquote align="center">
The explosiveness of dark waves
rotates and descends upon the chains
spawned by man's need to control,
Shipwrecked he is thrown into unknown
depths of consciousness forcing
him to forge below the surface
of his intellect—to unravel the irrationality
of it all.
</blockquote>

Rafael's favorite painting by Turner is *Shipwreck* (1805) because it shows his mastery of understanding the winds and tides by representing the sea and its vastness on canvas. In the midst of a sinking crew on a rescue boat about to be engulfed by an ominous wave, he depicts a group of fishermen in their boat attempting to rescue the drowning group. Even though man sometimes succumbs to destructive forces, there is a willingness in him that desires to help others in distress. This work oscillates with a poetic movement blending dark and rich colors with the images of men coming *cara a cara* with their own mortality. The revolving waves blend in obscurely with the dark grey of the sky's storm above. The synergistic effect generates a sense of wonder merging the conscious and unconscious worlds. It's almost like being in a dream state where the reality of the threatening sea awakens man from the comfort of sleep where the sea is calm with the reflection of the sun gleaming in all directions. This dichotomy between the destructive and constructive forces of Nature is one he must learn to accept and ponder its meaning.

MUSINGS ON CHECKMATE

RAFAEL OFTEN GATHERED with friends on the weekends to play chess. His closest friends, Gabriela and Marcelo, had just finished watching the film *The Queen's Gambit*. It was an intriguing story about an orphaned girl who was adopted and became a world champion by beating Garry Kasparov, the Russian chess master who was the world chess champion in 1985. The girl's name was Beth Harmon, and she was addicted to tranquilizers, which were given to all girls in the orphanage. Her addiction allowed her to envision a combination of chess moves on the ceiling of her bedroom. Beth was introduced to chess by the institution's janitor, and in no time it became evident she was a child prodigy of the game. Chess seems complex at first, but once a person learns how the pieces move, it becomes a little more simplified. But it does require a vast amount of patience and concentration; this is possibly why it is not attractive to many people. There are eight pawns in both the black and white sets of pieces. They initially can move forward one or two spaces. They attack other pieces diagonally one space at a time. Rafael thought the game was very philosophical.

The other pieces of each set are the queen and king. The objective is to place the opponent's king in checkmate, which means that the king is being attacked and cannot move in any direction because it will be taken by the opponent's piece. The queen is probably the most valuable because it can move in any direction—forward, backwards, diagonally and laterally one or multiple spaces at a time. Many times the queen can get lost in the mix of the game within the sixty-four spaces on the board with pieces scattered all over the place. What is so fascinating about the game of chess?

Gabriela had read somewhere that playing chess is like planning for a person's life. Once someone decides what his passion is, he makes moves to accomplish the steps necessary to fulfill that zeal. For example, if he decides to be a medical doctor, he graduates from high school and then goes to college. In college he will study biology and chemistry. He begins to set in motion his goal of becoming a doctor. Moreover, if a person resolves to run a sub-three hour marathon, he establishes a base of running maybe ten miles a week building up to eighty a week over a four to five-month period. Then, he incorporates speed work on the track or fartlek training (speed play), which are intervals of five, ten and fifteen minutes of fast running mixed with slow running in the same session. Plus, he also integrates proper nutrition, rest and strength training.

The objective of chess is to beat an opponent by making moves with the proper pieces to defeat his defense in competition. The castle is another piece, which is placed behind the pawns on the outer spaces of the board at each extremity. Each set has two castles. They move forwards and backwards or laterally, left to right one space or multiple spaces at a time. The beauty of the castles as well as the other pieces is that when they are moved precisely and correctly, there is a certain harmony involved. When things are balanced in a person's life, there is a coordinated balance. The sun rises every morning and sets every evening. Human beings wake up and go to sleep. If someone is sleep deprived, he does not function very well. Nutritionally, he requires a balanced diet of protein, carbohydrates and fat. This means he needs a blend of fruits, vegetables, meat, grains and plenty of water. As a human being, he feels good when he is physically active and maintains his body, mind and spirit fueled with the right "ingredients," whether this be meditation, food or rest. You can see this equilibrium in Nature with the rise and fall of the ocean tide and the different stages of the moon as well.

An equitable attack in chess allows a player to move each piece in unanimity with his other pieces, and it also permits the defending player to react to the moves of his opponent. Therefore, there is an action and reaction to each move. The concentration and patience become imperative because a competitor begins to see possibilities in the moves that follow. Just as someone reacts to things that happen to him in life, he also has to determine which action to take to resolve that issue. This is part of the art of attuning.

STAGNATED LOSS OF CURIOSITY

AFTER RAFAEL GRADUATED from graduate school in the fall of 1985, he and his former wife travelled to Toulouse, France to continue his doctoral studies. Rafael had minored in French, so he felt like he was prepared for the feat. During his studies, he was exposed to some of the classical artists like da Vinci, El Greco, Picasso and many others. What was fascinating then, once he boarded the plane from Houston, Texas to Paris, France, was that he would soon be visiting the Louvre, the most treasured museum in the world. The excitement of going to Europe for the first time was invigorating. That's what it must have felt like for Christopher Columbus and the hundreds of other explorers when they took off to sea to probe and conquer foreign lands in the fifteenth and sixteenth centuries. Rafael, like so many before him, left the familiar behind to search and learn about another country. He remembered saying to his taxi driver once they arrived to Paris, "Bonjour, monsieur. Nous voulons aller à notre hôtel dans les Champs-Élysées." After arriving to his small hotel on the iconic Champs-Élysées, he tried to find some clothing for his early morning run in his cramped quarters. Since he was not able to sleep much due to jet lag, he went for a run at 4 am. It was amazing to see the street cleaners out so early sweeping the asphalt with brooms and water. Water splashed from moving trucks as hundreds of workers cleaned the empty streets. As he ran towards the *Arc de Triomphe*, he relished the beauty of such a monument commemorating the victories of the French Revolution in 1789 and other armed victories by the French army. It was ordered to begin construction in 1806 by Napoléon I.

Reminiscing about his first trip to Europe, Rafael thought about the many people he had met and continues to meet who have no interest in travelling abroad to learn about other countries. As he witnessed the riot that took place this past week on January 6, 2021 in Washington at the U.S. State Capitol on national television, he viewed what seemed to be some extremists groups like the White supremacists charge the building demanding the cancellation of the certification of the presidential vote in favor of Joe Biden. After listening to an inflammatory speech by President Trump, who had been claiming for months that the presidential election was fraudulent and stolen from him, he encouraged the protestors to "fight like hell" to keep Congress from certifying the elections. Rafael wondered how many of those protesters, including the president, had been abroad. How many had tried to learn a foreign language and about the history of another country? Rafael thought of some of his in-laws who were Trump supporters and had no desire to visit Europe. How can a person have a broad understanding of politics and the global community if he has never gone overseas? His opinions are formed by the environment in which he has lived and grown up in. He cannot have an objective view of the complexities afflicting the U.S. and the world if he has only lived around family, spoken the same language all of his life and everyone around him looks the same.

Everyone must make it a point to view the *Mona Lisa* and other great works in person as he peruses the cafés of Paris, Madrid, Berlin and the museums of the world. So many Americans graduate from college without an appreciation of our past history and the cultures that formed the Western World. They are glued and chained by the technology of their cellphones searching for the mighty dollar to build their expansive fortresses and control the temperature, lights and locks of their homes with the touch and swipe of an icon on their phones. Democracy is eroding in America due to the cultural inertia and apathy of our society. It's a country that fought in World War II against the tyranny of Germany and Japan to protect the liberties of all free nations. Sadly, Americans, for the most part, are hedonistic and have lost their way in the valley of materialism like most advanced populaces of the world. Addicted to heroin, cocaine and every other drug a person can consume, more Americans per capita are slaves to addiction than any other country in the world. American society has enriched the pockets of drug cartels in Mexico, Latin America and elsewhere. No wonder many Americans can't overcome their racial biases that erode the core foundation of freedom, liberty and justice for all. Blacks kill Blacks in the inner cities of Chicago, New York, New Orleans, Los Angeles and other major cities. The killing of George Floyd in 2020 along with the hundreds of other Black men and women killed by the smoking guns of White police officers are woven into our daily psyche by local and national media outlets. Those with money live in separate racial enclaves where they are privileged to attend college if they desire to do so. The entitled White, Hispanic and Black communities graduate from universities to return to their respective "sanctuaries" to separate themselves from the underprivileged Whites, Blacks, Hispanics and other minorities of the U.S.

Universities in the U.S. have failed to truly educate their students. Professors are more interested in pontificating their ideas and publishing articles to attain tenure to serve as receptacles of dust like the books they write, but no one reads, that are stowed away in libraries under imposing cobwebs. Presidential candidates, like Mr. Trump and Mr. Biden, the Senate Minority Leader Mitch McConnell and the Speaker of the House Nancy Pelosi, who are in their late 70s and early 80s, must resign. It's time for them to retire to allow others who are more globally-minded and younger to lead our country. There is no doubt there is a lack of balance in our government as evidenced by the act of sedition America has recently witnessed.

According to Rafael and his friends White supremacists groups have evolved from small rural towns across the United States where the majority of the people are White. Rafael remembered coming to Whitesboro, Texas in the late summer of 1976 just after graduating from high school in San Juan, Puerto Rico. Bud Garnet picked him up at the Dallas Airport one hot afternoon in early July. He was accompanied by his wife Debbie who arrived in their dark maroon Bonneville car. They had a long-accented tone to their words, which were as long and drawn-out as the state of Texas. He was a farmer who worked the 100 acre lot belonging to Rafael's father whose mother was born and raised in Whitesboro. They were very friendly taking after the tradition of the Caddo Indigenous Tribes who originally lived in Texas. The word Texas is derived from the Caddo word *Tejas*, which means friendly. Rafael stayed with them for a month and a half before beginning school at Grayson County Jr. College in Sherman, a nearby town. Beneath the friendliness of many like Bud and Betty, Rafael sensed a deep-seated racism against Blacks and other foreigners. Rafael frequented the local businesses like the grain and feedstores along with many trips to the VFW Hall with Bud, and he never encountered anyone of color. Bud enjoyed drinking his gin and tonic with the local bartender and other townspeople he knew since childhood.

What became apparent to Rafael was the stagnation of small towns, especially when citizens did not leave the confines of their city limits. Working as a farmer is hard work as Rafael witnessed helping Bud bail hay and load the trailer with numerous bails. The intense Texas heat was crippling, and the fields were endless. The only contact Bud and some of his buddies had with a foreign culture, so to speak, was when they would go hunting in the fall and stay in a trailer they owned together in South Texas. When they weren't hunting, they would go barhopping where they would try to hook up with a young *señorita* prostitute. Sr. Garnet wanted to bring Rafael along to translate his desire for young Mexican ladies from his twanged English to Spanish. Rafael was amused by his foolish adventures to these cantinas. The older Texas personality was basically a good man shaped by his surroundings and culture.

Rafael and his friends surmised years later that White supremacists' attitudes evolve when there is a lack of diversity displayed in many communities across the United States and the world. When people don't travel to other communities or countries, a person's view of the world becomes warped and limited. Speaking another language, eating different foods and hearing foreign music, for example, are barriers that most are not willing to cross. It's uncomfortable to enter an unknown world where a person is not the center of attention and familiar to others. After the American Civil War in 1865, the Ku Klux Klan evolved for White-hate groups who couldn't stand the dismantling of slavery. The name was derived from the Greek word "Kuklos," which means "circle." The word Klan was added, and the members of the KKK say that it stands for White-racial brotherhood. The group was established in the South, and it convened secretly. It was intent on keeping Blacks in submission. They spread the vile evil and terrorism across the South by lynching innocent Black men and raping Black women.

How did this mindset of racism infest and grow in America, the land of freedom, justice and equality for all people regardless of their race? And why does the deep-seated hatred of others still exist today? When speaking to his wife Josefina, Rafael learned that she grew up saying: "A fight, a fight… between a n_ _ _ _ r and a White boy." This was appalling to Rafael and Josefina, now as adults, who are able to see how racial slurs are innocently spread into the consciousness of young innocent children playing in the playgrounds of Louisiana, for example. When groups of people like many Whites in the South and other rural areas of the U.S. are isolated, it becomes clear why many are racists. It's not to imply that all are racists, but someone can easily understand the nuances instilled in small communities, whether, for example, they are comprised primarily of Whites, Blacks, Hispanics or others. As adults many again don't venture outside of their city limits, and their lack of curiosity about the world outside of their narrow confinement is stifling. Their own fears of others have shackled them to a life of hatred and retreat. It's a cowardly way to live in a free and democratic society.

ELIMINATING POVERTY

RAFAEL'S THOUGHTS RETURNED to the game of chess as he thought about the bishops, which stand next to the castles on the left and right sides of the board. One bishop stands to the right of the queen, and the other one is next to the king. Once the pawn positioned in front of them moves forward, the bishop moves diagonally one or more spaces. It can move to the right or left; as a result, it is a very valuable piece. The beauty of the game centers on the fact that each player has all of these pieces at his disposal allowing him to strategize one move at a time or a sequence of moves played out in his mind in advance. Life is much like a chess game because an individual can plan his week or future one move or day at a time. A person has to be flexible enough to adapt to change. It amazed Rafael that one area most people ignore is finances. When he was in his late 30s, he was fascinated by mutual funds, individual retirement accounts and stocks. Even though the stock market goes up and down, if someone invests properly with a balanced portfolio between low-risk and high-risk securities, he can earn quite a bit of money. Now, that Rafael was 62 years old, he and Josefina had enough money saved to do whatever they wanted to do from now until the end of their lives. He no longer had to teach full-time; thus, he had chosen to work part-time as an interpreter. With the rest of his time, he enjoys lifting weights, training for triathlons, reading, writing and travelling. Additionally, he realizes now how beneficial it is to own three properties with no mortgages owed, which he now rents out.

The bishop can move one space or a maximum of five at any given time. It can be a metaphor for teaching people how to get out of poverty. If schools and parents would advise their children about investing at a young age, anyone could be a millionaire by the time they were 60 years old. For example, a young person could work his first job delivering papers for 50 customers. The newspaper pays him $25.00 a week, so he makes $100.00 a month. If he saves $10 dollars a month and eventually opens a savings account, he will have saved $120 in a year. In five years he will have accumulated $600.00. As his account grows, he can move his money into a money market account, which earns interest. From there he can begin to move some of his monetary investments into other types of financial assets like individual retirement accounts and mutual funds. The problem is that most children and adults spend more than they save. They can't wait to buy that expensive car, the luxurious home and fancy technological gadgets. Before they know it, they are in debt paying high interests on homes, cars and unpaid credit card balances. Now, they are in a financial hole.

How does the bishop relate to this concept of saving and eliminating poverty? The prudent player only moves his bishop or any piece with a purpose, which is to defeat the opponent in a fun way. Remember this is a game. If there is a piece like a castle or a pawn in its path, it may be wise to take that piece or not to do so. The same applies to finances. Rafael remembered years after a difficult divorce how fortunate he was to be able to sell a large home he and his ex-wife had built. He could have worked two or three jobs to try to pay the mortgage, but this would wreak havoc on his health and his other pursuits. So, he sold the house and paid cash for a smaller home. The rest of the money he kept in investments, and he also paid off the note on his fairly new truck. This was his very first financial test that woke him up to the realities of money and living responsibly. He also gained more freedom. He could have moved his bishop to capture the alluring queen of his opponent knowing he would risk losing his queen as well. Instead, he decided to adhere to the *circumlocutory method* of taking a pawn and keeping his queen and bishop intact.

There is always a way to make money in a weak economy. You could buy a used lawn mower and begin cutting grass. Before long this person could have 100 customers or more and charge a $50 minimum, depending on the size of the yard. The key to any business is to eliminate the overhead as much as possible. Obviously, if someone cuts the grass himself, he is going to make more money. If his business grows to 500 customers, then he can consider hiring some workers to help him. The other important decision is to save and invest the money he earns so that his profits multiply. This gives him the freedom to continue in this business or to do something completely different. He now has options and is not confined to one career path. Many doctors and other professionals go broke because they can't afford their luxurious office spaces and homes. They are not able to invest because they have more money going out than coming in.

Years ago Rafael remembered working as an adjunct instructor at three different institutions and earning about $30,000 a year. It was challenging because his yearly income fluctuated depending on the amount of classes he taught each year, which was directly related to student enrollment. In addition, he had to pay for his own medical insurance since part-time employees did not receive any benefits. He also realized academic institutions are very political, and administrators and professors, who are tenured, control the whole system. Adjunct faculty members are dispensable. It didn't take him long to realize the significance of diversifying and saving. One year he worked for a publishing company, Educational Testing Services, and made $56,000. At this time, he bought a new home for a little over $100,000 closer to his job in San Antonio, Texas. He only worked for this company for 1 1/2 years, but he earned enough to buy a new home and rent his other house. His position was going to be eliminated because federal funding for the program No Child Left Behind was running out. He worked as an Assessment Specialist creating tests for Puerto Rican children in the third, fifth and eighth grades. It was a fun job travelling to the Caribbean island and working with the teachers in Spanish.

Saving is imperative for eliminating poverty. Once a person is in a position to do the things he chooses to do, there is a lot of time to fill. Rafael decided he wanted to do some writing as well as to continue training and participating in triathlons. Money slips through a person's hands easily because he is not mindful of the things he buys. Like anything in life it requires discipline to control and be conscientious about money. But it is not something that is mastered once and for all. It requires constant attention and monitoring.

SANDRA AND TOULOUSE-LAUTREC

SANDRA WAS ONE of Rafael's good friends. She had just moved with her husband Frank to a town just outside of Austin, Texas from Baltimore. Sandra was a national level swimmer who had been competing since she was a teenager. Frank was a retired fireman and also a veteran of the Vietnam War. He suffered from post-traumatic stress disorder and depression. Sandra worked as a recreational therapist at the Methodist Specialty and Transplant Hospital in San Antonio, Texas. She was very involved with the Master's Swim Club, and Rafael met her one day while swimming at 6 am. Sandra had a slender body and an infectious smile. Her complimentary personality made it easy for her to make friends, and she was also a very good swimmer and very knowledgeable about the sport. Their friendship evolved over the years, and they became especially close for a period of time after Frank died from an overdose of heroin several years later. He had an addiction problem, but it had been under control for many years.

Sandra's father was a retired engineer who introduced her to swimming at a young age. Her Peruvian mother, now deceased, was a school teacher. Sandra spoke some Spanish and wanted to continue practicing the language with Rafael, knowing he was a Spanish teacher. For a short period of time, Rafael met with her and some of her coworkers during lunch at the cafeteria of the hospital in San Antonio where she worked. Rafael charged them each $150.00 for a total of 10 Spanish sessions. They learned vocabulary words related to their profession and chatted about everyday topics like family, travel, hobbies and other things. Rafael tried to focus more on their conversational skills. Sandra was more advanced than the others, so he would also have her read some short stories and discuss them with her. From time to time, she would write her own short story to share with Rafael. It was a fun time, one that he misses now.

Rafael's attention turned to his black bookshelf to the left of his desk with light from the outside represented by soft blocks of clarity displayed on the objects in his study. There he grabbed a book with a black glossy cover of Henri de Toulouse-Lautrec (1864-1901), the famous French artist. Art fascinated him even though he wasn't a "creative wizard" who worked with paint and brushes, but he liked to consider himself a *crafty designer* working with pen and paper. For him writing was the catalyst for expressing ideas and thoughts, a type of meditative trance that gave him the space to just be without physically doing. Plus, learning that Sandra's father was a painter made him turn his attention to art.

He learned that Toulouse-Lautrec was an aristocrat and also an alcoholic. Born in Albi, a town in the Southwest of France, he was attracted to the Parisian nightlife. Inbreeding was a negative side effect of this ancestry, which culminated in the marriage between his father and mother who were first cousins. Because of this, he suffered from a degenerative bone disease exacerbated by two falls in which he broke both thigh bones. Unfortunately, his leg bones never healed properly, and he walked around as a small disproportioned man who stumped around grotesquely with a cane. Art became his refuge. Everyone needs a sanctuary because, as a human being, everyone has a handicap. Toulouse-Lautrec eventually died of a stroke on September 9, 1901 due to his many bouts with hard drinking and a series of paralytic fits.

The one painting that stood out to Rafael was Lautrec's self-portrait (1880). The deep colors were magnificent (white, grey, brown and black). The richness of the colors stand out as he sits behind what appears to be a desk with many objects on it, such as candles in a holder, with one candle reflecting the other in what appears to be an Impressionistic mirror. His starched-white shirt was lost in thick brush strokes of white paint accentuated by the stiff collar and some sort of neckpiece, not your traditional tie. It appears to be like a scarf tucked into his shirt. His face is shaded as if to hide his true identity, and his torso is only exposed hiding his crippled legs behind the desk. There is a mantel piece that seems to be sustaining the canvas to which he is applying paint. It is a beautiful painting that captivated Rafael's attention.

The instinctive nature of the artist to compose a self-portrait is the same inherent need that writers have in exposing their thoughts on paper. It's a form of expression that needs to be explored. As a society, an individual lives and does without much self-reflection. He indulges in his compulsions or addictions, whether it be drinking, lusting and self-pleasing, exercising, working and many other activities. He is enlightened by a song, biblical verse or experience soon forgotten. A person must return to the *daily canvas* to create and invent. It's easy to become complacent in his accomplishments and then to fall into the monotony of living. The *virtuoso* repeats the same routine over and over again—waking up, eating, working and the multitude of other things he does. The question becomes: How does a person help himself and his fellow man? Rafael believed the answer was partially found in creating, meditating and recreating effectually. For the aging athlete, the motto becomes, "there is no finish line." A runner runs slower as he ages, but he must continue "flowing unceasingly" until the unremitting movement becomes a walk, and the walk becomes a crawl.

RUNNING TRANSFORMS

RAFAEL RECALLED GROWING up in San Juan, Puerto Rico. It was his junior year in high school, and he was running track. He remembered setting his alarm and waking up at 5:45 am every morning. Outside it was extremely dark, and the reticence of getting up disappeared once he splashed his face with cold water. He recalled the stiff-azure running shoes he wore. They were blue and had three white stripes on each side of the laces. It was normally pretty cool in the morning, maybe around 70 degrees. The stiffness in his legs transferred from his shoes would normally wear off after about 10 minutes of running. The streets were silent but slightly visible due to the lights above generating some luminescence every block or so. He didn't recollect exactly how he trained, but he tried to run pretty hard after warming up. The sweat would begin to lather on his forehead, and he could feel it dripping down his face. It was refreshing to see the first rays of sunlight rising above the streets and taciturn homes. This year he was training for the 1,500 and 3,000 meter races. There was something very satisfying about forcing himself out of the delightfulness of warm sheets to go out individually and run. Going against the grain of comfort to struggle and strive was an energizing feeling. That year he attended Robinson High School, and he was literally the only one on the track team running long-distance races. It was a small private school with approximately 300 students. There were some football players who ran some of the sprints and participated in some of the field events like the shot put and discus throw.

Reflecting on this moment, he thought about the present and his need to get outside and exercise on a daily basis now that he was older. There was a certain calling that beckoned him to be outdoors: the soft light in the morning, trees swaying in the slow breeze and the crispness of a new day.

"The Outdoors Beckons"

The morning calls us to stretch
in the midst of the dream world,
Transitioning from the assuage
of sleep we drift into the realm
of a beating hammer calling us
to enter the awoken world,
Time seems to escape swiftly from one
moment to the next,
The need to squeeze in a moment
of exercise to compete,
to paint with our minds the freedom
of Nature beckoning us to
join the tall standing trees, the creeks
dry from the lack of heaven's tears,
the dirt sticking to our tennis shoes,
We seek the outdoors to be alone
for a while before joining a society
in work, study and errands,
We take time to be truly human
before dehumanizing ourselves
in a world of activity and distractions.

This externalizing was as meaningful as internalizing. In a world that demands a person's attention and drains him of his true calling while earning a living to survive, many times he forgets the need to disengage and frolic alone or with others outside. Rafael was grateful for those "stiff-blue running shoes" with white stripes that waited for him to fill their being and carry him along those shadowy streets listening to the boisterous *gallo* (rooster) greet him joyfully at the dusk of day. That was a special time when the virgin light of his memory met the last strand of twilight from the previous night.

JUÁREZ AND IMMIGRATION

RAFAEL NOT ONLY reminisced about his personal past, but he also mused about the current issues of the day. With the new Joe Biden administration taking over the U.S. presidency on January 20, 2021, Rafael thought once more about the immigration crisis at the U.S. and Mexican border. He thought it was necessary to reflect on the accomplishments of Benito Juárez, and how his presidency would help the current U.S. policymakers better understand the immigration conundrum.

Benito Juárez was the only Mexican president of Indigenous descent, and he is considered the best one to have ever served in this official role. He was born in 1806 in San Pablo de Guelatao and died in 1872, and his parents were Zapotecs who died when he was three years old. He grew up working the land and caring for sheep; at the age of thirteen, he moved to the city of Oaxaca to enroll in high school. Juárez eventually graduated with a law degree in 1843 from the Institute of Art and Sciences in Oaxaca.

Responding to the immigration crisis at the southern border requires acknowledging and discussing the racial inequalities in Mexico. The majority of the population, 53 percent, is of Mestizo descent (a mixture of Indigenous and White European races) while White-Mexicans compose 9 percent and Mulattoes (a mixture of White and Black-African races) make up 5 percent. The elite class in Mexican society is comprised of lighter skin people; they have the most wealth and are the most educated. The largest ethnic group to illegally immigrate are the Mestizos who are the poorest and least apt to have the same working and educational opportunities as the White elites.

As the president of Mexico from 1858-1872, Juárez modified the Constitution of 1824 by advocating for human rights for the Indigenous and Mestizo segments of society. He created the Liberal Party that decreed the separation of church and state, and voting was to be opened up and expanded to all members of the public. In addition, he presided over the defeat of Napoléon III and the French in the battle of Puebla on May 5, 1862—thus, commemorating the Cinco de Mayo Holiday. Even though the French were defeated, more reinforcements arrived and the French forces were able to overthrow Mexico City. The French invaded Mexico because the Juárez regime discontinued the payment of a debt they owed the French because he and his Liberal Party were involved in a war with the Conservatives.

In 1863 Napoléon III invited Maximilian, the Archduke of Austria, to be emperor of Mexico. Maximilian accepted and arrived to Mexico in 1864. The French finally withdrew from Mexico in 1867 because the war was unpopular in France, and it was draining the French treasury. Maximilian was captured by Mexican forces and was eventually executed. This victory culminated in the last attempt by a foreign country to invade and interfere in Mexico and the rest of Latin America. Juárez was named *Benemérito de las Américas* (Distinguished One of the Americas) by Congress in the Dominican Republic for his commendable accomplishments.

It's significant to bring Juárez into the forefront of the immigration crisis because his achievements as an Indigenous president have been ignored for 149 years. Yes, lip service is given to him by establishing the Cinco de Mayo as a Mexican national holiday, but his service and prescience rest in the historical chambers of society where only the dust of corruption, economic and racial inequalities and political dominance of the Mexican White elite Conservative and Liberal Parties continue to prosper at the expense of the Mestizo and Mulatto people.

Unlike the current Black Lives Matter or the civil rights movement of the 1960s in the United States, Mexico has denied the racial inequalities that have exacerbated the immigration quandary at the border. There needs to be a more comprehensive awareness and movement in Mexico and the United States that also addresses the racial factors, a root cause of the immigration predicament that is commonly ignored, to honor the legacy of the *Benemérito* Juárez.

The continued or discontinued construction of the wall will not deter the mass exodus of Mestizos and many impoverished Indigenous groups from Mexico and other areas of Central America to the U.S. perimeter, but a more comprehensive and fundamental discussion of Mexico's history along with highlighting the accolades of Juárez will represent a beginning for dissecting the immigration upheaval that behooves the sharpest political minds. The current leaders in Mexico would prefer to maintain the current status quo while burying the heroic stratagems and vision of a humble Zapotec who leveled the economic and racial playing field for a short period of time in history. The United States could reference Benito Juárez in its efforts to revisit and revamp immigration reform for the betterment of all people and races, honoring inclusion and not exclusion, while dismantling the antiquated Mexican caste system and racial discriminatory practices.

MICHELANGELO'S DEPICTION OF THE SOUL

RAFAEL AND HIS friends, Carolina and Manuel, had a house party this past Friday celebrating the beginning of Mardi Gras. They would have a small gathering at Carolina's house, and they would enjoy shrimp gumbo, red beans and white rice along with a buffet of cheese, crackers and fruit. They limited the number of people attending because of COVID. Besides Rafael and his wife Josefina, Carolina and her husband Manuel along with Joe were the only ones invited. Carolina was an artist who specialized in *papel picado* (perforated paper) and had done several pieces of artwork for banks, restaurants and other establishments in the city of San Antonio, Texas.

As they all gathered around the dinner table with their glasses of wine and bottles of Abita beer, Carolina began talking about the work of Michelangelo, the famous fifteenth- and sixteenth-century Italian artist. She had been working on a project depicting Michelangelo's work of Noah and the Great Flood. What comes to mind in this painting is the chaos represented of nudes climbing a mountain, some attempting to uprear towards a lifeboat, others at the entrance of a home trying to find safe ground and, finally, a man with a long grey beard in the Ark with a handful of people getting ready to close the door before the water fills it up causing it to sink. In the center of the piece, a man is carrying a drunk Noah into the Ark, and in the upper left side of the painting, there is a tree with bare limbs leaning towards the people distressing in the unforgiving scene.

The three-dimensional painting allows the eye to appreciate the *flailing* water with the human forms *lumbering* against Nature and themselves. It is a life of continual deception and sin with no end in sight. The theme of slavery surfaces in its many forms: Man is slave to his sinful nature, man enslaves others and God enslaves man for his defiance and disobedience. The tree that appears could possibly be the tree of knowledge that has been forsaken and has lost all of its blossoms. Manuel observed that as someone grows from a child to an adult, he becomes more aware of his individuality. As a result, the needs of others become more foreign and distant. Without God man becomes trapped in his narcissism and is not able to empathize with others. It's a fine line for an individual to balance his needs and those of others.

Michelangelo has preserved many of the biblical accounts of our Western heritage on the ceiling of the Sistine Chapel in Rome. The flood represents the stressful periods of life a person will have to navigate and circumvent in his lifetime. Man is now living in an epic historical period, never experienced before in modern times, due to the devastating effects of the COVID-19 virus, which has killed millions of people around the globe. There are new strands of the virus evolving in parts of Europe as the Center of Disease Control begins to administer the necessary vaccines to the world's population beginning with the frailest and oldest segments of society. Paint and canvases are the tools used by the artist to preserve these images to learn about man's suffering throughout history. Art permits the viewer to see himself in the painting, which serves as a kind of mirror in which he witnesses his nakedness. Not only does the admirer notice the physical bodies, but the *bareness* of the "essence of being" becomes evident as well. It is the "eye of the soul" that attaches to its humaneness and weaknesses. By viewing these flaws in others, man can easily contemplate the imperfections within himself. Michelangelo's greatness is measured by his ability to create an art form that endures the test of time. It is as relevant today as it was to those affected by the flood in biblical times. This is what intrigued Carolina the most.

Rafael sat at his desk staring at the three inches of snow covering the grass in his front yard. San Antonio was under the grip of an arctic cold front that had blanketed the whole state of Texas with sub-30 degree weather for the last three days. There were power outages throughout the state since the frigid weather exhausted the energy sources capable of handling this type of extreme weather. Many areas were without water because many of the pumps were frozen, and the authorities had to wait for temperatures to warm up to make the necessary repairs. The grocery stores were only allowing limited purchases since trucks were not able to quickly restock shelves due to wintry interstates. It's been a trying time for the state of Texas. Rafael remembered some snow days in the past but nothing like this. It was a good time to reflect and muse about philosophy and society.

Even though the gyms were closed, Rafael was able to get outdoors to do some slow running/walking on the wet surface being cautious of the ice patches under shaded trees. In these sections he was able to run on the packed snow on the side of the road, which was crunchy but not slippery. The canopy of snow in the trees and shrubs was truly magical. He could really appreciate the beauty of the snow once he returned home and dressed after a warm shower. Luckily, he and Josefina had a gas water heater, so they were assured of having plenty of hot water to bathe. This was comforting along with the fact that they still had water.

The image of the snow and the silhouettes they formed on the branches, rooftops, mailboxes and shrubs were simply amazing. The snowflakes drifting in the air blown by the wind, the children making snowmen and the footprints of dogs left behind in the white ice mass were truly picturesque. The snow forces man to look from the inside of his warm home to the outside world just as he seeks the warmth of the inside after frolicking mirthfully in the frozen outdoors. The balance between physical activity and mental ruminations sustains his soul just like the need for cold and heat. Technology really distracts man from these essential elements he needs to strive to disentangle the constraints of becoming spiritually numb.

Just like Michelangelo desired to paint all of those scenes from the Bible, especially the depiction of God's finger touching man's *digitus index*. There is a connection a person seeks and needs. He wants to touch the snow to feel its purity and freshness just like he requires the solace of another human and God. Instead of watching T.V. all day or sitting in front of our phones drinking coffee and complaining of being bored, man needs something to compel him. Michelangelo needed his paint and brush to apply to the canvas to fully *realize* himself in his creation. He established a relationship between himself and Noah, for example. Noah was gathering mankind and the numerous animals to save them from the Flood. Michelangelo like Noah needed a purpose to *hallow* himself in the doldrums of existence. When he came face à face with Noah, he saw himself in a mirror. He saw the skin, bones and sinews of *his existential persona* characterized in the man clinging to a branch on the leafless and robeless tree as he held on so as not to drown in the ravaging deluge.

FINANCIAL SECURITY AND KLIMT

PEOPLE SEARCH TO save themselves from the ominous seething sea of consumerism that attempts to submerge them into the depths of debt. If someone considers the effect money has on him, he can easily notice how most are slaves to it. It is easier to spend money than to save it. Most people are not satisfied with just an iPhone because they want the latest model with all the bells and whistles. They want the most fashionable and newest car along with the biggest and most modern home. Saving and investing with the guidance of a financial advisor are the wisest things a person can do. Once his finances are in place with approximately one million dollars invested and if a person lives within his means, he should be able to do whatever he wants. Rafael also learned that owning a small amount of real estate, for example, is also beneficial as well. If a person has one or two homes whose mortgages are paid off, the rent collected from these properties could serve as liquid income to invest or spend on essentials like food, utilities and health insurance. But many people work jobs they don't enjoy laboring long hours while ignoring to eat properly, get enough sleep and exercise sufficiently.

In American society food preparation is often ignored. There are thousands of diets advertised to the public to help a person lose weight. But a healthy diet should consist of grains, eggs, fruits, vegetables, green and leafy salads, broiled or grilled fish, chicken, rice and some red meat.

Many Americans also deprive themselves of quality sleep. They think of it as a waste of time; therefore, they sleep fewer and fewer hours per night. Instead of getting seven to eight hours of sleep every night, they get between five to six hrs. Exercise is thrown into an individual's routine as an afterthought when it should be just as important as his work and family life. The body needs sustained exercise daily to rid it of toxins and stress. It also allows a person to get away in Nature if he chooses to walk, run, ride a bike, swim or engage in other activities. An hour of continuous movement liberates oxygen and blood to flow to all major organs and systems of the body. The body was meant to move and exercise and not to sit and eat.

In a society that is bombarded by advertisement and material success, people must learn to step away and not compare themselves to others. The reality is that there would not be a divide between the rich and the poor if everyone knew how to value and appreciate money. The young family that has too many babies before they are able to afford them sets themselves up for financial woes. The young doctor who buys a large practice and owns a big home while driving a luxurious car forges a foundation of financial insecurity. The mindset to becoming rich should center on putting some money aside from each paycheck. If a person earns $100.00 a week, ten to fifteen dollars should be invested in a savings or money market account. Once money begins to flow, he can consider investing in an individual retirement account, for example. It takes discipline and patience to build wealth, but everyone can do it. There is no reason to envy someone who is wealthy because anyone can acquire wealth. The only secret and principle to getting rich is to begin to save and let the interest in your savings grow over a long-term period.

It was early in the morning as Rafael sat in front of his computer looking through the shutters of the window and his life. The snow from a few days ago had completely melted. He reached over to the nearby bookshelf beckoning him to grab one of its books. He was drawn to the book displaying some of the works of Gustav Klimt (1862-1918), the well-known artist from Vienna. Along with Sigmund Freud who was

Viennese, Klimt became part of the Art Nouveau movement known for its "decadent" forms of art and literature. The tensions of the period fueled a juxtaposition in Freud's Vienna where Victorian morality mixed with the reckless pleasures of the day. Klimt's art celebrated the eroticism of women with an urge to fill the canvas with very intricate decorations.

Klimt was from the Viennese suburb of Baumgarten where his father emigrated to from Bohemia. His father worked as a gold engraver, but he failed to make ends meet. For this reason Gustav quit school at 14 but was able to enroll at a college of art and craft. He was very successful as he began working on commissions before graduating from college. Gustav formed a business partnership with his brother Ernst and Franz Matsch, another artist. They were hired to decorate the new public buildings being built in the 1880s and 1890s. In his 30s he established himself as a renowned painter-decorator of the flashy orthodox style of the period. Nevertheless, he grew weary of this art form and took part in the "rebellion against the establishment" leading to the creation of the Secession—a group of artists interested in more modern and adventurous styles.

The Secessionist maxim "to art its freedom" drove Klimt to place eroticism and, especially, women's bodies as the leitmotif of his art form. He diverted from the Viennese establishment's definition of nudity, which centered on the academic and idealized nude exemplified by the goddess Venus. His provocative illustrations of female nudity interjected an unconventional visual discourse of female sexuality into the public consciousness of his age. His work represented the liberating power of women's sexuality, which was curtailed and annihilated in the art establishment of his time.

Klimt spearheaded the forbidden form of the female body, and this was significant because he used art to defy the protocols of the established society of the nineteenth century to display women in a different light. Many times artists, writers, journalists and others see a societal convention, which is detrimental to the modernization of ideas, so they begin the process of challenging these views. This is not to say that artists, such as Klimt, contribute to the decadence and "promiscuity" of society even though this seems evident by some. Men and institutions like the Catholic Church have been notoriously licentious towards women and have been accused of pedophilia throughout history, but many of these immoral infractions have been covered up. They were not disclosed publicly because men and these types of institutions were more powerful politically than the women of the nineteenth-twentieth centuries.

In *Judith I*, Klimt depicts Judith, the biblical heroine who seduced and decapitated General Holofernes. It is known that Nebuchadnezzar, the Babylonian king, sent his General Holofernes to overtake the Jewish city of Bethulia. Judith, who was a gorgeous young widow, is determined to save the city by killing Holofernes with her own hands. She prays and wears her finest clothes to sexually entice him. When Holofernes becomes inebriated after drinking a lot of wine, she beheads him by using his own sword; thus, she wins a victory for the Israelites. Klimt accentuates Judith's piety, strength and voluptuous female features.

The observer also notices Klimt has fastened Judith's neck with a golden neckpiece, which seems to be purposefully very tight. It appears almost as if she is decapitating herself. The Viennese viewed this painting as being very scandalous and blasphemous since Judith represents a pious figure in the history of the Catholic Church. Her half-closed eyes, her exposed nipples and orgasmic smile were shocking to most. It is clear Klimt exposes a very erotic version of what transpired in this biblical narrative. His perspective opens up a new dimension and reality by emphasizing the *femme fatale*, which empowers the women in a primarily patriarchal society. She is now viewed as the "victor" who has the capacity not only to seduce men but to also impose her will over them. The depiction also raises the theme of life and death since Judith seems to be asphyxiating herself with the tight hold of the golden neck brace.

It could be that Klimt in this painting has "guillotined" the notion of women being submissive and pious. They are now liberated as the artist is to exhibit the sexual potency of the female and her powerful control over men. There is a fine line between the relationships between men and women, one that must be respected by both genders. Klimt realized like most artistic *virtuosos* do that the female body is attractive to the human eye, but instead of illustrating her as being very plump and unappealing, he constructs her in a way that is sexually alluring. This sexual liberation, so to speak, begins the process of men and women seeing each other in a different light. It also releases the woman to view herself as *unshackled* from the constraints imposed upon her from a male-dominated society. She is no longer the "object" of man's satisfaction, but man becomes the "thingamajig" of her control. As a result, men and women become more equal in this regard.

CREATING AND NERVOUS FATIGUE

RAFAEL, MARGARITA AND Carolina enjoyed talking about art and the influence it had on people throughout history. Many times great paintings as well as important written works are stored away on the forgotten shelves of libraries to be viewed occasionally by students doing research for an academic project. Rafael recalled a recent exchange he had with his uncle via email. He had sent his uncle a Christmas card in which his desire was to wish him a Happy Holidays and to also share the news of a recent book he had published, *A Jar of Clay*. His Uncle Tom never acknowledged the fact that he had published a book. It wasn't until Tom recently sent Rafael an email wishing him a happy birthday "with the rudderless rudeness devoid of any thoughtfulness and gentility" for purposefully not recognizing his book. Rafael responded by thanking him for the birthday cheer and by also mentioning he might be interested in his new highly acclaimed, at least in his mind, monograph..

Tom was incensed writing back that he didn't appreciate the advertising for Rafael's book during the Christmas holidays. After thinking about Bertrand Russell's book on happiness, Rafael thought about the notion of envy. Russell indicates that resentment is a component of unhappiness. Men envy the accomplishments of others. Rafael pushed the issue of his book because he felt his uncle was only interested in the superfluous aspects of relationships—only sending birthday and Christmas cards and contacting a person only when there was a natural disaster like the recent snowstorm in Texas that overpowered the power grid across the state, leaving many without power or water in subfreezing weather for days. These are important and necessary events to address and acknowledge, but there should also be an "intellectual component" to relationships. Many times this type of exchange is nonexistent when communicating with family or others.

As Rafael matured with his reveries and writings, he questioned the *raison d'être* of redacting. After releasing four books, many marketing companies have contacted him asking for a monetary price to advertise his works as if the sole purpose of writing is to make it to the bestseller's list.

Many family members and friends seemed incurious about his works. So, logically and emotionally, he questioned the purpose of his craft. He realized he wrote to satisfy a need within him to formulate and express his views. It became his *venue* for knowing and searching for the truth within, which many people in his opinion never do. The gift and experience of living afforded a person with this opportunity to just move through life without thinking or to maneuver through life by creating and deliberating for himself with the hope of having a dialogue, primarily with his veritable self but also with others.

In his book *The Conquest of Happiness,* Russell discusses the "nervous fatigue" that many feel in civilized society. Man is inundated by the constant hammering of a home being remodeled next door, the ubiquitous dings of his iPhone alerting him to the latest text or e-mail message, the hour commute to and from work and the never-ending activities that assault him from the first moment he wakes up until he closes his eyes at night. Many times he worries about issues he can't do anything about at the moment; therefore, he sabotages his sleep with these disruptive and intrusive ruminations. Russell reminds his reader of the importance of developing a disciplined mind. He suggests a person should think about things at their appropriate time. If, for example, someone needs to see a doctor due to a specific physical concern, he should call and make an appointment to see the physician the first thing in the morning. Once the time and date for his medical consultation is made, he should not worry about what the ailment might be. Think about something else. He should wait to speculate about his medical concern until he meets with his doctor on the specified day and time of his appointment.

Five years ago Rafael taught high school Spanish at a small town in South Texas. He would wake up every morning at 5:30 am, shower, shave, get dressed, eat breakfast, make his lunch, brush his teeth and leave by 6:40 am to arrive by 7:30. On the drive he would meditate as he watched the sunrise or grey clouds hang in the sky, or he would listen to music, which quieted his mind before entering the noisy domain of middle school students with their constant chatter and movement. One of his favorite songs was "Long Love" by Eric Clapton. It was a long composition lasting about 13 minutes. The individual riffs from each guitar note where particularly inspiring and contemplative. He thought about his long day ahead teaching seven classes of rowdy students, his short lunch period attempting to grade some papers and swallow down some lunch and his late afternoon workouts in which he would bicycle, run, swim or lift weights. Then, he would eat dinner at Bill Miller's, a well-known barbecue restaurant throughout Texas. He would return home to his newlywed wife at about 8:30 or 8:45 pm each night. It was a very hectic time.

There is no doubt he was experiencing the "nervous fatigue" Russell refers to in his writings. It was an exhausting time, and it came to a head a year and a half later when he decided enough was enough. One of his student's complained to the new and unseasoned principle about an incident that occurred in his class. The student talked and interrupted his class incessantly displaying a total lack of respect every day. Even though Rafael had talked to his mother numerous times, and he was disciplined often by spending his classroom time in the main office, it all came to a boiling point one day. Fed up, Rafael told the student to stop looking at him with that sarcastic expression on his face. Then,

Rafael sat at the opposite side of the room and stared the student down with a scary face, accentuating an open mouth and piercing eyes. The student was so scared he stormed out of the room, slammed the door shut and bolted to the main office. After school Rafael met with the principal and her aunt who worked as an administrator in the superintendent's office. Instead of listening to Rafael's account of the class incident, the administrator suspended him from school for a whole week. Rafael decided that he would no longer return to this toxic and vitriolic environment.

His nervous fatigue had reached its breaking point causing problems at home as well as at work. Now, that he looked back at the situation he realized it was due to the lack of sleep and continuous bombardment of noise and activities. There wasn't enough cushion to absorb the impact of the day-to-day issues that arose working in a junior high setting. Now, that he was semiretired working as a part-time interpreter, still training for triathlons and writing, he had a lot more time between the activities of his more balanced and relaxed lifestyle. There were other stresses he had to adapt to like having more time throughout the day. Sometimes he would start his activities a little late and then felt rushed to try to finish them. This is where the art of balancing comes into play even when a person is retired. Endless hours could be frittered away attending to hundreds of mindless activities and demands. It was necessary to be selective and disciplined in doing the essential things that motivate a person individually. Finding out what those pursuits are is the primary secret of his life.

Being around people with no purpose can be draining. Rafael thought about those who only travel to be doing something because they can't sit still and withstand a little monotony. He thought of those he knew who woke up, checked their e-mail and read the latest news of the day the first thing in the morning. He tried to envision those who worked to buy a bigger home with more technological gadgets to control the temperature, lights and every aspect of their lives. This was exhausting to think about, and it was a life he didn't want to live. More importantly, he didn't enjoy being around these types of individuals who didn't have a creative outlet or a strong purpose in life other than doing whatever Jack and Jane did over and over again. Purposefully living was not just about simplifying life as suggested by Henry David Thoreau, but it was more about finding the peace and intentional aspiration in each moment of living. For Rafael it was about creating, writing and investing in his own thoughts.

It is intellectual suicide to be persuaded only by the ideas and frenetic currents of the classics from the past or the *nouveau* scholars of the present. Individually, every person must wrestle with his own ideas and experiences realizing that he has the responsibility to carve out his own destiny in the dense foliage of living. The creativeness of humans never arrives but constantly eclipses, and the act of transcending allows him to re-create himself each day. The movement of *jittery* energy dissipates as he slows down to see, meditate and contemplate things. He must close off the external world to rest in the in-between space between the extrinsic and internal. It's the area where he can separate himself from what's known and unknown to dwell in the fog of these two extremes. This is where the writer must suffer and remain on the "trapeze" between complacency and innovative achievement.

RUSSELL'S AFFECTION

IT WAS A cool Monday morning in early March, and Rafael was sitting in front of his mind's eye looking through the drapes drawn by the stillness of his study. He was thinking about Russell's discussion of affection as it relates to human happiness. He gives the example of a man sailing along a stunning coastline on a sunny day admiring the beauty and placidity of his surroundings. The man feels a certain happiness provided by the security of his sailboat and the calm sea. He is looking outward as he perceives his elated state of being. On the other hand, another man's boat shipwrecks, and he has to abandon it to swim to the safety of the shore as the menacing waves crashed upon him. This person searches within and senses a deep insecurity for his life; therefore, lacks a feeling of security. He may experience a feeling of *felicity* once he is safe and reflects upon the danger he experienced. Russell uses these two examples to juxtapose the endearment a man and a woman may experience between one other.

A man may take the sentiment a woman gives him but may not reciprocate that love to her or vice versa. He or she may not interchange this love due to a deep-seeded insecurity or fear he or she may feel. This may stem from a fearful or diffident parent who taught the child that the world is a dangerous and menacing place. The child may have been brought up believing every dog will bite and every human being is evil. As a result, the child grows into adulthood with these deficiencies, which are sources of an underlying unhappiness. The child who is fostered in a more secure and loving environment where the world is not such a threatening place will overcome unexpected disasters more easily because his perception of fear is not exaggerated.

Rafael was grateful the fondness he shared with Josefina was genuine. They both loved each other equally, and they rendered their sentiments towards each other. This is not to say their relationship was perfect, but he realized it was essential to reflect on their partnership. Fear is an evil that affects all people, and it sometimes is avoided and buried away instead of being faced. In this respect, Rafael agreed with Russell in seeing how it can interfere with a person's happiness because a disquieted individual will take the endearment given to him and not return the needed love to his partner. There is a balance that must be established between being able to receive the love given and then return it to the other person, especially in the most intimate relationships between wives and husbands.

A sensitive human being must be conscious of the apprehension that causes the precariousness in his life in order to break that bond of doubt. In civilized societies a person escapes from dealing with these issues by immersing himself in his job or even his hobbies in an attempt to avoid confronting the affection he receives or does not obtain. It's necessary to be mindful of this because it can release him from the traps of a busy life where he becomes distracted by its frenetic pace and obstacles for clear thinking. Reading and writing force a person to come to terms with the elements that sustain a *heaven-sent* or unhappy existence. This way he is able to unravel and unpack the baggage of his own psyche to better understand himself. The whole purpose of contemplation is for someone to better understand and know himself in a world that forces him to do the opposite.

THE AGING ATHLETE GLIDING ON GRAVEL

YESTERDAY RAFAEL WENT out for a 6-mile run, and his intention was to run slow as he rested for a 5K race in a few days. After running the first three miles at a very comfortable pace, he wanted to run one mile at close to race pace, which these days at the age of 63 was about an 8:30 pace. The purpose of doing this was to accustom the body to running this fast in a race. He ran about an 8:25 pace, but he was really hoping he could go under eight minutes by ten seconds or so. The aging athlete has to accept that he will slow down over time. Thirty years ago he could run a mile under five minutes—his fastest being 4:47. He knew today that running that fast would never be possible again. Was this negative thinking? Of course it was not. It's just the reality of aging. On top of the acknowledgement of slowing down, he had been nursing a chronic Achilles tendinitis in his right foot for the past several years. It bothered him as he ran, and it would really flare up when he finished running. He treated it daily by stretching, administering cold and hot treatments and applying a topical steroid cream that soothed the aching. On some days it felt better than others. It was a constant balancing act to continue training and competing as he aged.

Thankfully, he combined his running with cycling and swimming along with weight lifting. Josefina, who is not a dedicated runner, talked about the difficulty she experienced running two miles now at the age of 65, which she would regularly do once or twice a week over the years.

She was an avid tennis player who also enjoyed swimming some. They both realized it was a process to come to terms with aging, one that every single person had to confront. Rafael also remembered reading in Russell's book that for many, especially the wealthy, it is burdensome to fill their leisure time with meaningful activities. It seems like many are consumed with boredom, and after travelling the world and eating the finest foods, this thrill wears off quickly. Rafael and Josefina were glad they had hobbies, like sports, along with work to give them a purpose in life. Rafael also enjoyed writing and felt like this was his calling to reflect and fill those monotonous moments of *subsistence* with an opportunity to create and direct his thoughts, distilling them in a meaningful labyrinth of discovery.

As Rafael thought about sports and his "history" as an amateur athlete, he realized it was time to become more flexible with his workouts. By this, he was becoming aware that it was no longer important to be concerned with how fast he could go, but it was more significant to feel healthy, rested and happy about competing. Coming to terms with the fact that he wasn't going to have the same energy levels as in the past was sometimes challenging to accept. The process was going to be painful, but the joy was going to be more intense in the long run. The same applied to writing in the sense that he sometimes wanted to have a larger pool of followers to read his books. It made him question the reason he wrote and published his own poetry and prose if not many people acknowledged his work. Like many writers, he questioned the logic behind this desire to continue scripting for his own sake and sanity and not for the recognition or approval he might receive from others.

These were the issues Rafael wanted to weigh and balance especially after his cycling accident over a year ago. The reality of the anesthesia flowing through his veins and the surgeon's scalpel slicing through the tender skin in the interior of his upper mouth, not once but twice, gave him a reason for looking at life a little differently. The fine counterpoise a person has to navigate daily is one he is aware of, or many times incognizant of, because of the matters he decides to face or ignore. The constant distractions of life can keep a person from dealing with these realities, and obviously each person defines his own truth. The human needs for working, eating, sleeping and taking care of himself are a constant obligation he encounters every day. The following poem came to mind during a sudden moment of enlightenment.

"Gravel Under My Wheel"

The white grainy pebbles blended into
my unconscious mind filling it with
a void of thoughts,
My lifeless body became one
with the hard and unforgiving
asphalt like paint dried on
the artist's canvas,
The daze of waking up like the
virgin blossom of a new petal
seeking to extend its feathery existence
out into an unknown world,
The eyes of another human looking
into mine wondering if I would
return to consciousness,
The dance in between the known
and unknown defined by the
slippery connection between rubber
and small pebbles shakes
my core,
A true blessing reminding me of the
fragility of life like a
seesaw of ups and downs,
Reminding me to write and observe
today because today will
be no more tomorrow.

It was Sunday, and Rafael thought about a 5K he ran yesterday morning in New Braunfels, Texas. He hadn't competed in very many shorter-distance runs over the last several years, so he thought it would be good to test his speed. The 5K is an interesting race because it is long enough to be a distance run but short enough to be a sprint. In other words, a person basically runs at full throttle the entire distance. Rafael covered the first mile in 7 mins. 52 secs, which he had not been able to do in a long time. He felt encouraged as the slightly wet asphalt from the drizzling rain caused all the runners to lose a firm grip with their shoes. The 2-mile marker seemed further away as he labored up a gradual incline in the grey-morning fog, finally reaching the marker in about 17 mins: 42 secs—still slightly under a 9-minute pace. He was really sucking air as a few runners slipped by him on the final mile. The intention was there, but he started to lose the group as the seconds ticked away. He finally realized he was about a half mile from the finish line. Along with a few other runners, he finally entered the back gate to the Rocky Beach Tube Rental establishment. The finish line could not come soon enough as he crossed it, grabbed his finisher's medal and bent over briefly gasping for air. His final time was about 28 mins 25 secs, and his pace was 9:10 secs per mile. It was a little slower than he had anticipated, but he was happy because he gave it his best.

His right Achilles tendon was screaming as he tried to remove his racing flats to put on his sandals. He struggled to balance himself since it was painful to stand on the affected leg. After wobbling over to the computer screen displaying the results, he noticed he finished 6th in his age group. He wasn't used to finishing this far down in competition, but it was a gentle reminder that there are still a lot of good older runners out there. As he drove through New Braunfels on his way back to San Antonio, he thought about the many runs and triathlons he had competed there over the 40-year span he had lived in Texas. The old bridge he went under right before Landa Park reminded him of the first time he went to Wurstfest, the traditional German festival overflowing with sausage and beer for its patrons celebrated every October. He was a sophomore at Southwest Texas State University, now Texas State University, and he recalled the crowd of hundreds of college students. The memory of kissing a couple of girls that night was one of his first introductions to Texas and the party atmosphere. As he reminisced, the throbbing ache from his foot increased bringing his thoughts back to the reality of the moment.

ART AS A CONDUIT FOR GOD

RAFAEL BEGAN PERUSING through the art book of John Constable, an English artist born in East Bergholt, Suffolk on June 11, 1776. He grew up in a middle class family with five other siblings. His father was a successful corn merchant, and at first, it seemed like John was going to follow in his father's footsteps. But John showed a passion for painting the countryside. In 1799 he gained his parent's permission to study art at the Royal Academy School in London. In 1802 he exhibited his first works at the Royal Academy. He preferred to paint landscapes creating *en pleine air*, meaning he wanted to paint outside in front of his subject in the fresh air. He differed from his contemporaries because he completed most of his work outside in one place, whereas others would begin in one location but finish their work somewhere else. For Constable his art was a means by which he conveyed ideas about morality and intellectual truth.

Constable met Maria Bicknell in 1809 in his home village. They fell in love in a short period but did not marry because he did not make enough money as an artist to support her. When his parents died, he inherited their legacy and an assured income. As a result, Maria and John married in London in 1816. The work that impressed Rafael the most was *Judges Walk, Hampstead* (1820). In 1819 Constable and Maria bought a house in Hampstead in a rural setting just outside of London.

They began a family there, which grew to seven, and these were the happiest days of his life with Maria.

The painting *Judges Walk, Hampstead* depicts a dirt path running through a densely decorated patch of trees. The colors of the leaves are a dark green and black sprinkled with red from the setting sun. The pathway along with the shadows imprinted by the trees are drenched in red and orange. Sitting there quietly looking at the image, Rafael imagined John and Maria walking peacefully soaking in the cool air and enjoying the serene panorama. Rafael's thoughts turned towards the love his father Nizael had for Puerto Rico and the beach in Isla Verde. Nizael's disciplined routine of walking along the emerald waters of the Caribbean Sea and swimming in its refreshing embrace reminded Rafael of the rituals that connect us spiritually to God.

Artists like Constable dwell in a unique place, which forces them to sit in front of their subject. In this case Constable settles in front of a patch of trees soaking in the brilliant hues, the movement and subtle nuances of leaves bristling in the soft wind and calm rays of the nocturnal sunset. He searches for the correct balance of colors to form the shapes and perspectives he sees. The artist also connects with his feelings by establishing a bond between himself and the natural world. This serves as a conduit to communicate with God, the one who pursues the seeker in the quietness and enticing beauty of the outdoors. The path represents the walkway man takes as a human being traversing this world. As a sentient being, he observes, feels and moves towards God.

Constable like all artists must unravel the mysteries and nuances of the motif in front of him. The tree has an existence of its own that it shares with humans and all critters of this world. Saplings and Nature allow man to think peacefully as he strolls or sits quietly under them. He can see the squirrel frolic from branch to branch, and he listens intently to the yellow-headed woodpecker chop away at the tree's bark. Its resilience is noticeable when the wind strongly forces itself upon its branches and limbs, or when the thickness of its canopy of leaves provides a comfortable shade to enjoy in the midst of the intense summer heat. The artist needs this time to separate himself from the *busyness* of life to become God's instrument for playing the "music" given to him freely to perform on his canvas. In a world too preoccupied with living and doing, he needs that *elusive* space to settle within himself to combine brushstrokes, mixing shapes and forms with a plethora of colors.

SELF-DISCOVERY

THE ARTIST MUCH like the writer cannot perform his craft with the sole purpose of selling his canvas or book. It's really not essential if his art ever sells or if his book is ever read. After writing several books, Rafael was inundated by calls from literary agents wanting him to change his book covers and have them republished by a better known publishing house. They all asked the same question: "Don't you want to sell your books to make a lot of money?" Of course, authors want to sell their work, but this should not be the main factor that motivates them to write. Writing for Rafael is time he could spend in solitude with his thoughts—communicating with God, so to speak. It gave him an opportunity to take letters and words to produce something unique, original and personal for his own individual growth.

In school you learn the basics of grammar and sentence structure. Students are exposed to literary material where they have to comprehend and infer the meaning of a story, essay or novel. These are necessary skills to assimilate in order to advance to the next grade level, to graduate and find a good and satisfying job. Authors write much like sailors sail their vessels because it gives them meaning. Writing and painting are exercises in discipline in which the artists express their uniquely inherent thoughts on a canvas or piece of paper. Their intent is not to become the next Picasso or Shakespeare but to become the individual they are meant to be according to their own rules and perceptions.

As Rafael became older and had more time for leisure, he soon realized how the monotony of life can really sink in during the free time available to him. After or before a busy day, he cherished the time he could carve away alone with his computer and thoughts. Minutes and hours sometimes could be spent in front of the T.V. or browsing through the daily newspaper watching and reading about others. But writing afforded him the time to observe, react and respond to his inner world, a special place that constantly evolves and changes. It's the internal dwelling that society most ignores because people are programmed to do and complete one task after another. People are consumed by their lists of things to do in order to scratch each activity off their agenda; once it's accomplished, they add another item to their never-ending list. Rafael, as a writer, wanted to stop and take a different path to use his art form as a tool of self-discovery to journey along a spiritual pilgrimage towards the light of God. He wrote in order to find God in this linear passage from birth to death.

THE DICHOTOMY OF EL SALVADOR'S COFFEE BEAN

OFTENTIMES, DURING DINNER Josefina and Rafael would talk about some of the current events they had read about in the local newspaper. Lately, much had been reported on the immigration issue. Rafael observed that many U.S. politicians are overwhelmed by the immigration crisis at the southern border with Mexico. As thousands of unaccompanied children and adults from Central America converge into detention centers across Texas, Arizona and California, few analysts discuss the root causes of the mass migration. It's imperative to focus primarily on the gangs that evolved from the excesses and "extortion" of the Salvadorian coffee plantations and the wealthy.

Few policy makers make the connection between the coffee oligarchy or the "golden bean" era of El Salvador that emerged in the early twentieth century until its demise in 1929 due to the stock market crash and the emergence of gangs dominating the communities of present day El Salvador. The Salvadorian economy totally tanked at this time. Approximately 14 families controlled the coffee industry, an elite class, composed of two percent of the population, which profited from its production while ninety-eight percent of the population (Indigenous and low-wage workers) gained no earnings. The extreme poverty would be the seed that fertilized the ground for emerging gangs later on.

In 1932 Augustín Farabundo Martí, a socialist activist, led an army of poor Indigenous and peasants against the elites who controlled the army. The revolt resulted in the massacre of 30,000 indigent Salvadorians. The uprising was the result of anti-vagrancy laws, which kept and *still* keep the laborers of the coffee plantations from moving around to find other types of work and depriving them of the means to purchase and own their own small parcel of land.

From 1932 to the 1970s numerous authoritarian presidents selected by the *supernal-satanic class self-consumed in avarice* presided over the country. In 1972 the majority voted for José Duarte from the newly formed Christian Democratic Party. Ruthlessly, the supernal class drowning in their dreams of extreme greed stole his election and denied him power. Duarte was arrested, tortured and exiled to Venezuela by the army and National Guard. In 1979 the *Junta Revolucionaria de Gobierno* (JRG) was formed, and it was a government entity composed of civilian and military officials from the Left and the Right.

The JRG assassinated the Archbishop Óscar Romero of San Salvador while he was conducting mass in 1980 because he had continually denounced the JRG's repressive measures for some time. Furthermore, the JRG forced the resignation of all civilians from its government enclave, and it became a right-wing dictatorship. The last straw occurred when JRG snippers murdered 42 people mourning the death of Romero.

The *Frente Farabundo Martí para la Liberación Nacional* (FMLN), the same group that rose against the elite in the 1930s, surfaced again fighting in a protracted civil war (1980-1992). The U.S. backed the JRC with money and military training while Cuba aided the FMLN as part of the Cold War between the U.S. and the Soviet Union. A total of 75,000 lives were lost as a result of the conflict.

During the civil war many Salvadorians immigrated to Los Angeles during the 1980s, and it was here where the young men and women formed their own gangs like the MS-13 and its counterpart the Barrio

18 to protect themselves from other *pandillas* like the White Fence that already existed in L.A. After the Salvadoran Civil War ended in 1992, the MS-13 and the Barrio 18 members were deported back to El Salvador, Honduras and Guatemala. Since 40 percent of the Salvadorians were displaced and numerous homes were destroyed, the instability became "virgin soil" for these gangs to flourish.

By understanding and discussing this segment of El Salvador's history, U.S. policy makers can legislate for better immigration reforms that pressure the Salvadorian elite and government to take more responsibility by sponsoring and funding more programs to prevent and rehabilitate the gang members who overwhelm and overflow the prisons and control the communities of this small Central American country. The U.S. and the international community can assist in helping to build a better judicial, social and economic infrastructure that encourages the Central American elite, *the satanic-cupidity class,* supported by the present-day Biden-Harris-Obama-Ocasio-Cortez's machine of evil, represented by the United States' ignoramus liberal political-monolingual-racist 2024 Democratic Party, to share their wealth instead of drowning others in their greedy thirst that took root with the "golden bean monopoly" of the early twentieth century. The U.S. can learn that "diplomatic Band-Aids" like the wall or detention centers are not long-lasting solutions to this immigration conundrum at the southern border.

A MISSED OPPORTUNITY FOR DIPLOMATIC UNITY AND COOPERATION

JOSEFINA NOTED EL Salvador had an opportunity to unite with Honduras, Nicaragua and Guatemala at the beginning of the twentieth century, but the elite classes of each country decided to remain independent from one another. Today this idea of becoming united could possibly pose as an initial step towards ending the gang and high crime concerns in these countries. There has to be pressure from the international community to coerce these nations to establish anti-corruption commissions to help rid their governments, militaries and police forces of their blatant corruption and repression of the poor. These Central American states and their leaders should also be persuaded to unite, so they could combine their economic resources along with their political agendas to tackle these gang-infested locales.

Instead of focusing on the *mano dura* (hard hand) approach of cracking down on the bosses and members of the MS-13 and Barrio 18 and of filling up every crevice of their limited prisons, government officials could develop a plethora of preventative measures that could lure vulnerable youth into other types of employment, so they could earn a living and become honest and hardworking citizens of the Northern Triangle countries (NTC) of El Salvador, Honduras and Guatemala. Most money could be invested into building better schools and vocational centers where they could learn and become productive citizens.

The present incompetent director of Homeland Security, Alejandro N. Mayorkas, has been instrumental in abetting and aiding the corruption and disfunction of the MS-13 and other Cartel organizations in all of Mexico, Latin and Central America. Sadly, Mayorkas should be in prison for supporting and encouraging the worst form of slavery ever in the history of mankind: the sexual and abusive sex trade and trafficking of small and innocent children as depicted in the movie *Sound of Freedom*. Vice-president Harris and President Biden along with their partner in crime *Tonto* Mayorkas support this horrific sex trafficking of innocent children of God from those Hispanic countries mentioned above south of the border due to them completely opening the southern *parameters* in Texas, Arizona and California. The vulnerable Spanish speaking *younger ones* of God are despicably abused sexually by the plethora of pedophiles, primarily in the U.S., and throughout the world.

This is the result of the liberal Democratic machine, with no knowledge of Spanish and no interest in learning about the historical past of these Spanish speaking countries to better understand and assimilate the political and cultural *identities* of their rich traditional tapestry.

The Biden-Mayorkas open border policy and the complete disregard for the law pertaining to legal immigration and the uplifting of Title 42 in February of 2024, before the next presidential election in November of this year 2024, is a complete disgrace and lack of any kind of brain power for ever ameliorating the Satanic approval of the unconscionable EXPLOITATION of Hispanic minors for dirty and filthy American men and women pedophiles spilling their evil orgasmic SEED of disgust for their carnal devilish satisfaction. Hunter Biden also supports this type of sexual immorality along with his lies involving the extortion of millions from Russia and the multitude of other countries in that Asiatic region of the world, including China.

It clearly states in the Bible, Revelation 21:8: But as for the cowardly, the faithless, the detestable, as for murderers, *the sexually immoral,* sorcerers, idolaters, and all liars, their portion will be consigned to the lake that burns with fire and sulfur, which is the second death. In addition, Mark 9:42 underscores this truth of the whole Biden administration and family, specifically Hunter Biden, as expressed in his adamant untruths and uncontrollable-sexual-carnal corruption and strong and blinding addiction to *the needle of cocaine*: Whoever causes one of these little ones who believe in me to sin, it would be better for him if a great millstone were hung around his neck, and he were thrown into the sea.

Clearly, all men and women globally, including me the author of this book, fall short of God's Glory. However, the Biden- Harris administration of evil and the devilish Mayorkas purposefully and willfully accelerate their *political vehicle* full-blast and full-throttle with the determined intention to distastefully and satanically support with fervor a completely and unapologetically open border and for trafficking of the innocent, vulnerable and precious children along with the illegal distribution of fentanyl from China, which has killed thousands of American children and numerous more globally.

This must stop now, and President Biden and his son Hunter along with Vice-President Harris, and Mayorkas must be impeached, imprisoned; in my opinion, metaphorically hung with God's great millstone and thrown into the deepest sections of the Gulf Sea and Rio Grande River. As the author, I don't claim to be Jesus as the politicians just mentioned proclaim to be as evidenced by their satanic and godless policies they support and create in the world they lead.

In addition, a small U.S. and international military and police presence could be sent to these Central American areas to help train their military and police forces in confronting the violence devised by gang violence by instituting a ubiquitous presence with nonviolent outsourcers (specialized schools and vocational training centers) to reduce the escalation of crime. These forces could possibly establish relationships with these criminal syndicates to help them reestablish themselves within society as productive citizens. Members from these illicit organizations could be offered opportunities to earn wages after enrolling in vocational institutions that offer courses in mechanics, carpentry, plumbing, electricity and other essential jobs. Foreign companies from the U.S. and other parts of the world could invest in building factories requiring workers to work with solar panels, electrical cars and lithium batteries, wind turbines, computers and other environment-friendly forms of work.

Establishing the conversation with these southern countries in need is the key to finding solutions. The knee-jerk reaction of erecting a higher and impenetrable "barricade" along the southern border along with building more detention centers for the illegal people crossing the *Río Bravo* is not the answer. The root causes of the immigration crisis like the previous example delineated in El Salvador is one that is rarely discussed because the American public and the majority of its politicians are not informed nor are they intuitive enough to dig a little deeper to discover where this "cancer" started.

The U.S. has always lacked the diplomatic forte to deal politically with countries like El Salvador. The U.S. and European markets became the primary consumers of the coffee boom of the early twentieth century in this Central American country. The industrialized nations contributed to the repression by the Salvadorian elites of the Indigenous laborers who worked the coffee plantations. Americans as a whole need to be more aware internationally of their direct and indirect contributions to poverty throughout the world, especially the countries to the south of our shared border with Mexico.

GUATEMALA SOLD ITS AGRICULTURAL SOUL

AS RAFAEL THOUGHT about the plight of the Central American people, he perused the history of Guatemala where he learned about Juan José Arévalo, the first president to ever be elected fairly by winning 85 percent of the popular vote. This is basically unheard of in any Central or Latin American country. He served as president from 1945-1951; not only was he a good politician, but he was a great educator as well. Arévalo attended *Escuela Normal Central para Varones* where he graduated with a teaching degree in 1922. He dedicated himself to writing, and he authored his first textbook, which was used for reading in all the institutions and schools throughout Guatemala. Arévalo received a government scholarship to study at the *Universidad Nacional de La Plata* in Argentina where he earned a Ph.D. in philosophy in 1934. He also met Elisa Martínez, who eventually became his wife, in Argentina.

On May 13, 1947, *la Ley de Emisión del Pensamiento* (law of free thought) was proclaimed in Guatemala. Censorship was now prohibited and free thought was then instated. According to Rafael and Josefina, this was a huge accomplishment by Arévalo's administration. Arévalo espoused the concept of *socialismo espiritual* (spiritual socialism), which many international governments, including the U.S., equated to communism. But Arévalo opposed the Conservatives who believed in keeping Guatemala under the colonial rule where the government and Church oppressed the poor Indigenous populations under their feudal system. Liberalism evolved in 1821 at the end of the War of Independence from Spain. The Liberal Party differed only in its rhetoric from the Conservatives claiming it supported the human rights and freedoms of all people, but the reality was they were just as repressive towards the poor and working class as their conservative counterparts.

Arévalo's "spiritual socialism," as defined in the article composed on October 31, 1944 of *La República* newspaper, was a doctrine of moral and psychological liberation where an individual is free to gain economic as well as spiritual freedom. The hatred and oppression towards the lower-working class can no longer be tolerated in a republic that wants to progress and be concerned about the welfare of all of its citizens. The "liberal selfishness" of the past two centuries must be superseded by the generous immersion of the individual in the collective being. He states that communism, fascism and Nazism were also socialist, but it was a socialism that would feed man with the left hand while it mutilated his moral and civil rights with the right hand.

Arévalo's government decreed the Work Code on February 20, 1947, which granted rights to workers to be paid a decent wage for the work they performed. Before this law was enacted, property owners, especially the large coffee plantation landowners, forced the poor Indigenous and Mestizo populations to work without pay during the Great Depression of the 1930s, which affected the whole world. If the worker did not want to toil in the fields or if he did not desire to work on road constructions, so agricultural products could be transported to major markets and ports, they were imprisoned. This was the first law ever signed in Guatemala that protected the rights of the peon. His government also created the Guatemalan Institute of Social Security, the Central American and Panamanian Institute of Nutrition, the Faculty of Humanities at the Guatemalan University of San Carlos and the Institute of Anthropology and History. He also initiated the construction of the National Library and General Archives of the Government, known as the General Archive of Central America of the National Conservatory of Music. Under his administration the Guatemalan Ballet, the National Symphonic Orchestra and the National Choir were reorganized.

Before Arévalo, General Jorge Ubico Castañeda was the dictator of Guatemala from 1931-1944. When Ubico was in power, he granted land to the United Fruit Company (UFCO), which was exempt from paying taxes and allowed to pay low wages to workers. Guatemala became known as one of the many banana republics. The UFCO eventually became the owners of the Guatemalan train system, and it owned 50 percent of the fertile land of which only 2.6 percent was used to cultivate agricultural products (primarily bananas). Ubico instituted two laws that oppressed the Indigenous and Mestizo working class. The first law, known as the law of *viabilidad*, forced peasants to work 30 days a year constructing national highways. The second law, known as *la Ley de vagancia*, forced the laborer to work a certain number of days a year on the land of wealthy landowners. There was no legislation at this time that defended the rights of the laborer. Furthermore, the autonomy of the universities was suppressed, and all secondary schools were militarized. In 1943 the *Asociación de Estudiantes Universitarios* (AEU), Association of University Students, was founded. In June of 1944, the initial revolution began against Ubico's dictatorship. Ubico stepped down on July 1, 1944 as a result of the strikes organized by the university students due to his unpopularity.

When President Jacobo Árbenz Guzmán was elected president in 1951, he proposed a program to distribute some of Guatemala's unused land to peasants who were landless. The elites (2.2 percent of the population) owned over 70 percent of Guatemala's land. In addition, the UFCO owned quite a bit of the untouched land and complained to the U.S. Government that Guatemala had turned to communism. After the United States convinced the American population Guatemala was a Soviet "satellite," the CIA led a coup to overthrow Árbenz in 1954; he was replaced with Colonel Castillo Armas, a dictator more aligned to the interests of the UFCO.

Árbenz realized ownership and control of land for the peasants was Guatemala's number one economic issue because there was no industry. Illiteracy was rampant with 70 percent of the population not able to read or write, and 80 percent was barely able to survive economically in the countryside. The Guatemalan soil was extremely fertile, but only 2 percent of the landowners owned 72 percent of the cultivable land. Only a small part of their property was being developed. In 1952 Árbenz and the Guatemalan Congress passed Decree 900, which ordered the expropriation of all ownership of land larger than 600 acres and not being tilled.. These confiscated properties were to be partitioned among the landless peasants. The landowners would be compensated based on the assessed tax value of the land and would be paid with 25-year-government bonds. Meanwhile, the peasants could obtain low-interest-government loans to pay for their lots. This decree affected the monopoly of the UFCO, which owned 600,000 acres of mostly unused land.

To make matters worse, Árbenz left UFCO officials flabbergasted when he confiscated a large chunk of the company's land and offered to pay a compensation of $1.2 million based on the tax value created by the group's own accounting department. The U.S. State Department and UFCO demanded $16 million, which Árbenz refused to pay. Secretary of State John Foster Dulles and CIA Director and brother Allen Welsh Dulles, both former partners of the UFCO's main law firm in Washington, convinced President Eisenhower that Árbenz had to step down. Accepting their concerns, Eisenhower authorized the CIA to organize "Operation Success," which took place in June of 1954 to overthrow Árbenz militarily. The CIA selected Colonel Carlos Castillo Armas to organize and execute the coup.

After gaining control and power, Castillo quickly outlawed more than 500 trade unions, the UFCO regained more than 1.5 million acres of land and other big landowners recovered their land as well.

Unfortunately, this marked the end of Guatemala's short-lived-democratic experience. Guatemalans were exposed to government terror for the next four decades, more than any other country in the modern history of Latin America. Death squad victims were kidnapped and killed on a regular basis. Helicopters dropped mutilated bodies into crowded stadiums to keep the people terrified, and anyone who asked about "vanished" loved ones had their tongues cut out.

Rafael and Josefina contemplated these historical facts, but it was difficult to just blame the political avarice, pugnacity, and "huffiness" of the United States. There is no doubt that critics are justified in seeing the role the Eisenhower administration played along with the UFCO in creating a banana republic in Guatemala, but it is also necessary to hold the Guatemalan elite and past dictators like Ubico and Castillo responsible for conceding and becoming puppets of the United States. The "covetousness" and the racism against the Indigenous Mayans and poor Afro Guatemalan laborers existed in Guatemala, El Salvador, Honduras, Nicaragua and Costa Rica long before the U.S. extended its militaristic and bellicose footprint in these countries. Árbenz and Arévalo tried to do what no other leader and not even the Church attempted to do by leveling the playing field for all. In a way, the exploitation of the UFCO and the U.S. Government opened the door to drug cartels and gangs that now riddle the majority of these Central American countries. Rafael believed that the only hope for these countries is for an international community, headed by the U.S., to institute martial law and establish free elections by the people. The Central American elite should be forced to pay money by means of taxes and new legislative laws for the government to redistribute the land and protect the rights of all of its citizens, build more schools, and force banks to provide low-interest-rate loans for peasants and other poor laborers.

THE HONDURAN ENIGMA BAFFLES THE U.S.

IT'S ALSO NECESSARY to discuss briefly the situation in Honduras that further complicates the plight of many to the U.S. border. President Biden's immigration reform policy must apply political pressure to the current Honduran administration under the leadership of Juan Orlando Hernández. The U.S. with the aid of the worldwide community should consider a decree of "international martial law" since the Honduran Government refuses to make the necessary reforms to combat organized crime and provide better educational opportunities and jobs for the poor Indigenous and Mestizo populations. Finishing the construction of the wall and building more detention centers across the U.S. are the failures of U.S. policy makers who ignore the root causes of the Honduran immigration crisis. The current Honduran administration along with the "snobbery" of the affluent elitists are content with the status quo because their pockets continue to overflow with Honduran *lempiras* while the poor seek their fortune of "crumbs" fallen from the failed policies of Honduras and the U.S. To better understand the plight of Hondurans to the U.S. border, it's imperative to examine the main reasons for this massive wave of immigrants moving north.

Cristopher Columbus discovered Honduras on his fourth and last voyage to the New World in 1502 when it became a colony of Spain.

The country was named Honduras, which means deep, because the first Spanish conquistadores noticed how fathomless the oceans where along its coasts. The exodus of many Hondurans, primarily the poor Indigenous and Mestizos, "metaphorically" began in the sixteenth century due to the forced labor the Spanish imposed on them establishing deplorable human rights violations that continue to this day due mainly to the failed *Provincias Unidas de Centroamérica* (United Provinces of Central America) and the *República Federal de Centroamérica* (Federal Republic of C.A.) from 1824-1838. The incompetent and corrupt government officials like the current President Orlando Hernández are also the cause.

The Honduran flag contains five stars representative of the united and federal republic comprising the countries of El Salvador, Guatemala, Honduras, Nicaragua and Costa Rica when Mexico and the rest of Central and South America became independent from Spain during the War of Independence (1810-1821). The Central American union separated from Mexico and formed their own federation in 1824.

The "united experiment" fell short because of the animosity that existed between the Spanish elite, *superiores desdeñosos* (arrogant superiors), and the *criollos* (Spaniards born in Central America) that developed from the sixteenth to the early nineteenth centuries. General Francisco Morazán (leader of the Liberal Party) triumphed against Manuel José Arce (leader of the Conservative Party) in the first Central American Civil War (1826-1829), and instead of setting up free elections, Morazán allowed the old Spanish authorities to rule so he could remain in power. Historically, the fundamental error that Mozarán committed was the failure to distribute the land and property of the Church and oligarchy among the Indigenous masses and to elevate them to citizens with full rights. He ruled over the indigent Indigenous tribes and Afro Central Americans as a dictator from 1830-1840.

The further inability of General Morazán to unite the Liberal and Conservative Parties led to the dissolution of the Federal Republic during the Civil War of 1838-1840. He also missed the opportunity to democratize the republic by not uniting the Indigenous people as mentioned previously. At the end of the war, the republic split and one by one each country (El Salvador, Guatemala, Honduras, Nicaragua and Costa Rica) became independent from each other.

Furthermore, Orlando Hernández, who is currently serving his second term as president of Honduras, is accused of gaining the presidency by voter fraud. There are also allegations of corruption and connections with organized crime. Hernández appointed General José David Aguilar Morán as the director of the police department. It is reported Morán assisted Wilter Blanco, a drug lord who is serving a prison term in the U.S., in transporting millions of dollars' worth of cocaine throughout the country.

The initial "enslaving chains" of the Spaniards and the failed Honduran state along with the illicit government headed by Hernández and other factors not discussed here: the exploitation of a plethora of other authoritarian rulers in Honduras along with the imperialist vestiges of the United Fruit Company from the U.S. [1910-1970] and the devastation of Honduras's infrastructure by Hurricane Mitch in 1998 are the germinating seeds culminating in the colossal departure of Hondurans to the border between the U.S. and Mexico.

A comprehensive examination of these historical and current imprints must be part of the blueprint for U.S. politicians as they discuss immigration reform. It should include an all-inclusive approach involving Honduras, the rest of Central America and Mexico along with the universal community and the U.S. Political pressure must be applied to the current Honduran administration and their *recherché* class from the outside world to reform and eliminate the corruption, crime and oppression of its poor. This must begin with a multinational council that guarantees free elections for all of its citizens while protecting their human rights to work and prosper. If the current Honduran administration does not cooperate in this effort, international martial law must be invoked immediately. The global community must unshackle the immigrants from the initial historical and current "chokeholds" buried and ignored by government officials determining their fate as these vulnerable fleeing souls trickle through the porous rampart at the border.

AUSTIN'S FORGOTTEN DIPLOMACY

KNOWN AS THE "Founding Father of Texas," Stephen F. Austin negotiated a law with Spain and then Mexico to allow 300 Anglo-American families to settle in Texas in 1822. His Father Moses received approval from Spain for this land grant but died soon after; Mexico had just gained its independence from Spain after a long war lasting from 1810 to 1821. Spain was interested in developing the land in Texas since there were more illegal Anglo colonists settling there than there were Spanish citizens. Stephen F. Austin founded the city of San Felipe de Austin nestled along the Brazos River in 1824. The river was originally named *Los Brazos de Dios* (The Arms of God) by the Spaniards.

Not only was Austin an *empresario* (businessman/land contractor), but he was also a lawyer. Moreover, he realized the significance of learning Spanish in order to negotiate with the Mexican Federal Government. He bought a Spanish grammar book, *Gramática de la lengua española compuesta (Spanish Language Grammar Composition)*, and taught himself to speak and write in Spanish. The majority of the Anglo settlers refused to learn the dominant Spanish language even though they had agreed to do so as Mexican citizens acquiring land in Texas.

As the new Biden presidential administration takes the helm, it seems like one of the foreign-policy strategies for effectively dealing with the immigration crisis would be to appoint bilingual officials who can speak Spanish and English to negotiate with the current Mexican President Andrés Manuel López Obrador in Spanish. When Austin travelled to Mexico City in 1822 to speak to the Mexican congressional committee to draw up a colonization law for the new Anglo colonists during the presidency of Emperor Agustín de Iturbide, he spoke in Spanish. He didn't ask them, "¿Hablas inglés? Do you speak English?" His success was due not only to his diplomatic finesse but also to his ability and willingness to speak Spanish, which demonstrated his respect for Mexican culture, as the National Colonization Law was signed in 1824 along with the Coahuila and Texas State Colonization Law in 1825.

It is even annotated historically that a Comanche war party had stolen some horse saddles belonging to Austin and some of his men as they stopped to camp one night. Eventually, Austin met up with the Comanche chief, who spoke some Spanish as well, since his Indigenous tribe had learned the importance of speaking this language when trading with Mexican citizens. Austin spoke some Spanish and knew a few Comanche words, which allowed him to regain some of the stolen items and prevent a fight. His Spanish grammar book was among the items he never recovered, but he acquired a new one soon afterwards.

Eventually, Austin was jailed in Mexico City for suspicion of treason in encouraging the Texan colonists to revolt, which was not the case. Imprisoned for eight months in 1835 under the presidency of Antonio López de Santa Anna, he kept a journal in Spanish writing letters to Mexican officials assuring them of his desire to abide by the Mexican laws and Constitution of 1824. When Santa Anna became the dictator of Mexico, relationships deteriorated between the Texians and Mexico's new regime. Once Austin was released from prison and joined the Texas Revolution, the Texian Army defeated the Mexican troops during the Battle of San Jacinto on April 21, 1836.

A person can only speculate, but it might be accurate to affirm the creation of Texas would never have occurred without Austin's linguistic prescience. Those initial land grants may have been denied, and a large "wall" could have been built keeping the "illegal" Anglo settlers out if he had not purchased that book. It could be beneficial for American officials and governors, especially like Governor Greg Abbott in Texas, to follow the example of Stephen F. Austin by purchasing a "Spanish grammar book" in an attempt to ameliorate the immigration crisis at the border. Austin's influence and historical contributions were so valuable that the seat of government of the great state of Texas resides in Austin, named after this trailblazing figure.

SUFFERING AND PARADOXICAL THINKING

PUTTING HISTORY AND politics aside, Rafael began rereading *Further Along the Road Less Travelled* by Scott Peck in which Peck discusses "neurotic suffering" versus "existential suffering." He references the societal introduction of Freud's theories, which were misinterpreted by many. Many parents tried to raise "guilt free" children, and that is why there are so many people in prisons because the majority of inmates feel no shame for the crimes they committed. Peck believed an individual needed to experience a certain amount of guilt to distinguish right from wrong. He referred to this as existential guilt, which is healthy. On the other hand, neurotic suffering was excessive guilt where someone carried too much guilt. A person, in this instance, could feel culpable about everything. For example, he could experience being at fault for not calling someone on his birthday or because he did not ask someone how his sick family member was doing. According to Peck, everyone must go through the "desert of suffering" to grow. If a person is not traveling through the wasteland, he is stifled.

Many times it is easier to stay stuck in a place of comfort instead of growing and reaching beyond a person's limits. One of the areas for Rafael to "stretch existentially" pertained to his athletic life. As he aged, he realized he could no longer run as fast as he used to be able to do. He often looked back and remembered the past where he could run a 4:47 mile, and now it was difficult to run a sub 9-minute mile.

By travelling through this desert at the age of 63, Rafael is learning to realize that everyone is approaching mortality. This is undeniable, and his slower times are a reminder of this truth. The practice of "metaphysical guilt" allows the mind, body and spirit to see the enlightenment of the good struggle and not to become obsessed with the despair of not accepting the unstoppable fact that every person is moving forward towards death. The key is to keep moving instead of giving up the athletic lifestyle. An athlete constantly has to come to the realization that it takes the body a longer time to recover from a hard workout. Many times the effort seems just as hard as twenty years ago, but when he looks down at his watch, he sees the difference in a much slower time. This can become a joyful realization instead of an agonizing one.

All of this thinking led Rafael to read *The Portable Jung* about the life and work of Carl Gustav Jung. Jung believed there were four functions of the psyche: sensation, feeling, thinking and intuition. Many times, according to Jung, man can become stuck in a neurotic state when he only tries to solve a problem by only thinking, feeling, being aware of the sensation or intuiting. Jung would suggest he incorporate all of these four functions when solving or dealing with an issue. He also underlines the significance of paradoxical thinking. Where there is light there is darkness. Where there is health there is illness. Where there is good there is evil. Where there is life there is death. Where there is consciousness there is unconsciousness. Furthermore, Jung believes that all humans are born in the *unconscious state*; while in this disposition of the mind, there are no problems. Animals live in a natural environment in which consciousness does not exist. Jung relates this to the tree of knowledge where Adam and Eve become conscious when they eat the forbidden fruit. Before doing so, they lived in a state of unconsciousness.

It's interesting Jung uses the image of the sun and its cycle to explain consciousness and unconsciousness. When the sun begins to rise each morning cognizance begins to appear until its full fruition or brilliance at noon. This period from sunrise to noon represents the stage of life from the time man is born until he reaches 40 years of age. From noon until nightfall is when consciousness begins to fade into the unconscious world. From noon until nightfall symbolizes the second half of man's life from the time he is 40 years old until his death. The night is equivalent to the unconscious world, which is more mysterious. During the peak of consciousness, Jung suggests that a person as a human begins to form his identity by choosing a profession and doing all the things necessary for establishing his place and well-being in life. But from the age of 40 and beyond, man should be more concerned about himself and his inner life as he lets go of the striving and becomes more contemplative about the remaining years of his existence.

THE EGO AND LOVE CONUNDRUM

RAFAEL WAS ALSO intrigued by Wayne W. Dyer's *Your Sacred Self* in which he discusses among many topics the difference between the inner and external worlds of each person. The ego is part of the external world that depends on the fear of things that might happen or what others might think of someone. Fear feeds on performance, and if an individual fails at something, there is a feeling of unworthiness. Love defeats fear, according to Dyer, because God is love, and love is God. Love is not reliant on performance or how big of a house a person has. Neither is love dependent on how someone views others but on how he views himself. A loving person is interested in others and less interested in himself.

Rafael and Josefina reminisced about a recent trip they took to Isla Verde, Puerto Rico with Rafael's elderly parents Nizael and Cynthia who were in their mid-eighties. While walking the beach, they noticed the numerous women in string bikinis taking pictures of themselves in many sexually-suggestive poses with their phones. It was so comical to see this blatant need to photograph themselves as it were a photo shoot for a Sports Illustrated swimsuit edition. Now Rafael could see the fear of not appearing beautiful and the need of seeking self-appraisal by posting their pictures on their Facebook page. The amount of insecurity people feel is based on fear and not love. A person would naturally think the opposite of fear is courage, but in actuality, Rafael and Josefina believed the opposite of fear is love. Why is love so difficult for a human being to obtain?

The ego, according to Dyer, tells a person to ignore the internal life of the spirit. It is in constant need of acceptance preventing someone from loving himself just as he is. Humans have a need to be respected and liked. People become engrossed in how they look, what kind of car they drive and house they have. Women or men, who are divorced, many times feel unloved and worthless. They feel like they need another man or woman to love them because they have never experienced the love from within that does not dwell on what they don't have. The inner life of the soul is the only way to experience affection because an individual's purpose in life is not to have someone love him but for him to show fondness towards others. If a writer, for instance, writes in order to gain fame, he has failed as an author. He will never be satisfied unless he realizes he only creates to fulfill a need inside to love himself and to do what he yearns to do. The ego wants to be recognized, but love does not care about recognition.

The art of balancing becomes significant because man realizes there are many opposites: fear and love, love and hate, possessions and nonpossessions, lightness and darkness and many other dualities. The ego wants man to possess things, the more the better. It is never satisfied. It wants people to hate and fight with each other. It wants people to feel superior to others. Love wants man to create and establish lives of peace and tranquility with himself and others. It prefers the light over the darkness of the soul. Love takes away the need to seek and acquire more things, and it does not differentiate between those who are superior to others or to those who are rich or poor. Love is existential, whereas the ego is materialistic.

CONVERSATIONS DRINKING CAFÉ YAUCONO ON A SATURDAY

IT WAS A Saturday morning, and Rafael and Josefina were sitting at their dining room table soaking in the early morning sun as it filtered through the stained glass windows. They both had a fresh cup of *Yaucono* coffee, which they had purchased in Isla Verde, Puerto Rico. They took Rafael's elderly parents Nizael and Cynthia to their favorite beach. Nizael never wanted to leave the island, but it was necessary for them to be close to their family in San Antonio, Texas. Rafael and Josefina walked with them several times on the soft-silky sand of this magical Caribbean island. It was necessary to keep an eye on them since their gaits were unsteady. Rafael walked with Cynthia as Josefina went ahead with Nizael. Nizael's favorite strip of beach was about 1.25 miles long accented by the convergence of golden sunlight with the sea's deep blueness and the sand's bubbly softness embracing his toes. He usually liked to walk to the end of the Isla Verde Cemetery where he would stop and get in the water to swim about 50 yards. Nizael began to enter the water with Jan right behind him. There were some very small waves, which concentered with him as he progressed forward. He suddenly stopped and turned around because he felt it was too dangerous for him. Rafael realized then it was Nizael's way of saying goodbye to his best friend, the Caribbean Sea at his favorite beach. Rafael remembered watching Nizael over the years jumping right in beyond the waves and doing his 50-yd. swim. Rafael felt joy and sadness at the same time. It was a beautiful experience to witness.

Rafael's attention shifted to trying to understand the root causes of the immigration crisis at the southern border. Most journalists, such as Mike Bailey who was the editor of op-eds for the *San Antonio Express News*, continued to run pieces only discussing detention centers, the separation of families, asylum reform and whether to continue building the wall.

However, Rafael preferred to focus on the main sources of this conundrum at the border. He turned his attention to Colombia and the dictatorship of Gustavo Rojas Pinilla from 1953-1957. His dictatorship was the most "civilized" and least repressive of the Latin American continent. Furthermore, it was the only dictatorship that existed in Colombia, which was also considered the most democratic of the southern continent. Pinilla and the Liberal and Conservative elites were concerned there was an *enemigo interno* (internal enemy) among the urban as well as the rural locals. This enemy was communism, and the fear was that it was spreading throughout Central and Latin America during the Cold War. Colombia had a close relationship with the United States since they sent approximately 2,000 Colombians to fight alongside Americans during the Korean War (1950-53). They were the only Latin American nation to send soldiers to this war. They were known as the *Batallón Colombia*.

On June 13, 1953, General Rojas overthrew the Conservative government of Laureano Gómez by means of a military coup d'état. Gómez was incapable of detaining the Liberal guerrillas from El Llano under the leadership of Guadalupe Salcedo and the lawyer José Alvear Restrepo. In the south of Tolima, a communist guerrilla was growing and gaining power. The Communist Party in Colombia took root during the presidency of Luis Mariano Ospina Pérez (1946-1950) using the slogan *autodefensa de masas* (self-defense of the masses). Once the guerrillas were crushed, Rojas Pinilla offered them a pardon if they agreed to turn in their weapons. The guerrillas influenced by the Liberals opted to do this, but the communist guerrillas, primarily from the regions of Cundinamarca and Tolima, chose to demobilize and not turn in their weapons. Furthermore, on June 13, 1954 Pinilla enacted the 1823 decree that granted amnesty to all those who committed political crimes before January 1, 1954. However, Coronel Eduardo Villamil, a former commander from Antioquia who fought against the dictatorship, filed documents that revealed a concentration camp for those who fought against Pinilla's military. In these camps like the one in Araracuara, the inmates where treated worse than animals and were confined to a life of misery.

It's interesting to note Rojas Pinilla's dictatorship only lasted four years, and he did resign when both the Liberals and Conservatives pressured him to do so. Even though Pinilla did some atrocious things, such as torturing leaders of guerrillas that opposed him, having his military kill many student protestors objecting to his policies and incorporating concentration camps, he did accomplish many positive things such as building new highways, schools, hospitals and universities. He also helped establish the infrastructure for television, radio and other forms of communication. Pinilla also brought relative peace to his country, and there was little interference from the U.S. during his time in office.

Rafael believed that the U.S. has never looked at Central and Latin America holistically. On June 7, 2021, Vice President Kamala Harris was in Guatemala and then travelled to Mexico City the next day to visit with government officials there to discuss the "root causes" of the immigration crisis at the southern border of the U.S. Unfortunately, she does not speak Spanish, and the only word she knows is *pendejo*, which means stupid and can also mean asshole.

Vice President Harris, of Indian and Jamaican descent, failed miserably in her recent two-day trip to Guatemala and Mexico to discuss anything of substance pertaining to the border crisis. Instead of addressing the corruption of the government and the elite, the past history of dictatorships, gang violence and the endemic racism against the Indigenous citizens of these countries, she made the following statement to the poor Indigenous and Mestizo immigrants: "Do not come to the U.S."

Here we go again with another American politician who does not speak Spanish and does not know how to apply diplomatic pressure on Central American and Mexican presidents. The latter prefer American officials like Harris, who do not know Spanish, because they are in a better position to be manipulated. Just imagine for a moment, if Harris would have said to the Guatemalan and Mexican presidents, Alejandro Giammattei and Andrés Manuel López Obrador: "Estoy agradecida de estar en su país para discutir la corrupción que existe aquí dentro de su administración y entre la élite guatemalteca y mexicana". (I'm grateful to be here in your country to discuss the corruption that exists here within your administration and among the Guatemalan and Mexican elites.) Even if she had read such a statement, it would have had a profound effect on opening the door for a discussion on immigration.

AMERICAN CORONA BEER ATTITUDE AND DIPLOMACY

MANY AMERICANS, POLITICIANS and citizens often believe that learning a foreign language like Spanish is inconsequential. Many fulfill the foreign language requirement to graduate from high school and college. Rafael observed this first hand as a teacher and instructor of Spanish for many years at the high school and college levels. The main attitude of most students is "Hey, I just want to pass this class. Why do you give us activities in class to speak the language? I'm not going to a foreign country like Mexico, and if I do, I just need to know *cerveza*."

Rafael thought this attitude towards foreign languages permeated the American psyche. In his latest trip to San Juan, Puerto Rico, this came to the forefront again. He was having dinner in Isla Verde with Josefina at an outside beach restaurant with tables and chairs on the golden sand of this island's pristine Caribbean Sea. In the background he could hear the boisterous sounds of American tourists speaking English spiced with alcohol with their voices dissipating in the soft breeze of the dark night. Rafael's reminiscing thoughts drifted to the Spanish *conquistadores* who encountered the native *Taínos* in their initial encounter in the fifteenth century on this same island with its *arena de oro* (golden sand).

When politicians like Harris and everyday American citizens don't learn or attempt to speak, in this case, Spanish, they disrespect the people of Guatemala, Mexico and Puerto Rico. It shows a contempt for their history, culture and traditions. It's a sign of ignorance and egomania where others view Americans as self-centered and self-righteous. This foresight becomes especially pronounced when American politicians or citizens visit a foreign country and, yes, speak English only.

The image of American diplomacy is best captured in Snoop Dogg's Corona commercials where he raps in English as he walks and then sits with his cold *cerveza* on a chair in white sand and turquoise water lapping the shoreline. The statement: La vida más fina (the finest life) is penned with the emblem of Corona. We all enjoy a cold and fresh *cerveza* on a beautiful beach, but unfortunately, this "foaming diplomacy from a frosted glass" will not solve the immigration crisis at the southern border.

This past week Rafael remembered an incident when he was having an island tabletop delivered to his home to be placed in his kitchen. It was black with a white granite decorated with grey and black markings throughout the marble. It was actually a Silestone quartz countertop, which beautifully matched the counter surface by the kitchen sink and other work areas by the stove. Two men delivered the *island*, and they happened to be from a small town outside of Tegucigalpa, Honduras. He spoke to them in Spanish, and their faces lit up when they heard native Spanish flowing from Rafael's *gringo* mouth. Rafael asked them about the political situation in Honduras where there is obviously a lot of gang violence and corruption among the jobbery politicians and the *haut monde* (high society). Juan Orlando Hernández is the current Honduran president. The younger gentleman did agree there was a lot of malfeasance in his country. He stated Hernández did actually arrest and prosecute some of the major Honduran drug lords so that his brother Juan Antonio Hernández Alvarado, a convicted drug trafficker, would have less competition among the dealers of the underworld. How about that for a Honduran president? No wonder so many are fleeing the country to come to the U.S. The Honduran man also mentioned that, during a recent election, a major candidate was winning when there was a power outage; when the power returned, Orlando Hernández, who was previously behind in the vote count, was suddenly ahead.

Rafael also discussed the recent trip Vice President Harris made to Guatemala and Mexico where she only spent one day in each country. The question Rafael and the Honduran man asked, "Why didn't she visit Honduras and El Salvador where most of the immigrants are from?" Her trip probably did more harm than good. The man did not know Mrs. Harris did not speak Spanish. This is totally absurd to visit a foreign country in Central America to discuss the root causes of the immigration crisis and not speak the language. In this short conversation Rafael had with these Hondurans, he learned more about the main seeds of the aforementioned immigration *imbroglio* than any politician or academician who studies the problems abroad from dusted textbooks and journals and from the English lens of the U.S. looking out into the unknown world of Central America. People would think inconsequential-unconscious President Biden who is a "people's person" would understand the importance of speaking Spanish. This way he could have conversations with people he meets in their native language. The younger Honduran man also described a major drug lord who was his next door neighbor, and how he used to see him arrive to a local bank in his neighborhood with an entourage of ten cars to laundry money. He would see them come in with bags of cash.

BLACKS ENSLAVED BLACKS BEFORE BEING SHIPPED TO AMERICA

IN CONJUNCTION WITH the immigration crisis at the southern border, American politicians are beset in the quagmire of only seeing the race problem from the perspective of Blacks and Whites. Americans can't seem to heal from the scar slavery has left on its culture. The corruption and violence in Central American countries will continue to get worse, and this criminal syndicate will eventually spill over more dramatically and significantly into the U.S. This point is further exemplified in the article "Alamo's slavery link not remembered," published in the San Antonio Express News on June 26, 2021. The author Julián Olivares, an Emeritus Hispanicist at the University of Houston, states that "[t]hose who died with valor and sacrificed at the Alamo did so in defense of liberty and slavery." What is wrong with his point of view?

When slavery is discussed, specifically between White slave owners in the U.S. and Blacks brought over from Africa, Rafael believed it was necessary to discuss the Blacks in Africa who enslaved other Black Africans. Blacks brought Blacks to Africa's western coast and sold them to European slave merchants who transported them to the New World. The majority of the slaves sold to Europeans had been slaves in Africa. They were free people who were captured in wars from different regions of Africa or were enslaved for committing a crime. In Senegambia, the Guinea Coast and the Slave Coast of West Africa, captives from wars became the main source of slavery. In Angola subjects were kidnapped or condemned for debt, and in most cases merchants did not sell people from their own tribe. They sold people they regarded as aliens. Africans did not think of themselves as Africans but as members of different tribes within the African continent.

It's also necessary to consider the perspective of the Apologists who argue that European traders did not enslave anyone. They actually bought Africans who had already been enslaved and who otherwise would have been killed; therefore, they claim that the transatlantic slave trade actually saved a lot of people. There is some truth to this, but there is no denying the European slave merchants did actually invade some villages to capture Africans. However, most European countries like England, France, Denmark, Holland and Portugal set up bases before the end of the seventeenth century along West Africa's coast where they bought slaves from Africans in exchange for weapons and other goods. Furthermore, some societies, such as Benin in southern Nigeria, did not sell slaves. But others, such as Dahomey, specialized in enslavement, and in other areas, such as Asante in present-day Ghana and the Yoruba in western Nigeria, natives were engaged in warfare that created at least half of all slaves from the eighteenth and early nineteenth centuries. Many African rulers sold slaves not only for firearms but for textiles, alcohol and other rare imports.

Rafael and Josefina wondered why most Americans ignore the Black-on-Black perspective when they are presented with the views of Black Lives Matter, critical race theory (CRT), defunding the police and possibly the speeches of Martin Luther King, Jr. In his declamation "I Have a Dream," he could have referenced the slavery that existed in Africa, specifically Blacks on Blacks. Obviously, this was wrong, but it needs to be mentioned because most Americans believe that slavery was an institution spawned by Whites in the United States only. However, a person could argue Blacks begot slavery in Africa. So, basically, Blacks and Whites are to blame for the creation of slavery. The media, politicians and many academics refuse to address both sides of the slavery issue, which is one, if not the main catalyst, of the underlying causes of racism in America. Most Americans isolate themselves within the four walls of the U.S., so even though they live in a world interconnected by the internet and travel, they are mainly monolingual and have a "mono-slavery" viewpoint when it comes to critically thinking about this historical imprint on their nation.

AMERICA'S INDIFFERENCE

A COUNTRY LIKE the U.S. is influenced by its educational system and its overall culture that looks within and does not look without. When a country as a whole assimilates to the American way by speaking only one language, interests in other foreign countries diminishes. It's hard to determine why most Americans are like this. Rafael and Josefina have a friend named Cristal who seems oblivious to the world outside of herself. She's been married a few times and is now dating someone from Utah. Her boyfriend works in Colorado as a construction foreman for high-rise buildings. When they get together once every couple of months, Cristal only talks about what she has been doing and about accomplishing her next task. There seems to be no interest on her part in politics or international events. She really doesn't have the ability to ask questions about what other people are doing. It's almost as if she lives for the next photo op where she can post something on Facebook. Cristal has been retired now for a couple of years and has enough money to do the things she enjoys doing. This seems to be a common trend among most Americans or people in general from developed countries.

In another incident Rafael remembered a conversation with Tomás who works as a bicycle mechanic at a local bike shop. Evidently, Tomás earned quite a bit of money as a professional triathlete, but he is now retired and works at the shop for fun. He was showing Rafael pictures of a 75-meter Olympic-size pool he is building at his home in Boerne, just outside of San Antonio. He is installing special LED lights, and he's also going to build a waterfall close to the pool. Tomás went on to describe the bar he'll have adjacent to the pool along with a high-tech sound system. Plus, he will have a vine bush grow over a wood structure to cover his cars in a carport facing the road. Rafael stated, "Man, you're not going to be able to retire now since you'll be in debt." Tomás seemed slightly irritated by his response since Rafael was not that impressed. Tomás retorted back, "Jesus never retired. I'll keep working forever." Again, there is nothing wrong with buying nice things and making additions to a person's home. But Rafael believed when that becomes the focal point of someone's life, it seems to separate him from others and the world. Instead of becoming a "citizen of the world," a person becomes a "creature" between the four walls created by and for himself. This is a shame in a world where people and countries depend on each other.

Josefina noted another article in the local paper by Paul Krugman in which he discussed the critical race theory (CRT), which seemed to be a chic topic. Yes, there have been many racial atrocities committed throughout American history like the Tulsa Race Massacre of 1921 where a White mob killed successful Black residents and destroyed their homes and businesses, and the 1938 Federal Housing Administration Underwriting Manual affirmed different racial populations should not live in the same communities. What the Left and Right seem to ignore, or they just don't have sufficient knowledge in regard to this issue, is that this supposedly CRT exists everywhere in the world. If a person reflects on what's happening in Ethiopia, he can see this theory being played out before his own eyes. Abiy Ahmed, the prime minister of Ethiopia, is trying to maintain order in the midst of growing unrest and political tensions. Several opposition parties were upset because the March elections this past year were postponed due to Covid-19 restrictions. National elections are supposed to take place sometime this year, but so far they haven't. In addition, the popular Oromo singer, Hachalu Hundessa, was assassinated on June 29, 2020. All of this has led to civil unrest and violence. The Ethiopian National Defense and Oromia regional police forces have carried out violent counterinsurgency operations throughout the western and southern Oromia regions. Many Oromo civilians, including medical professionals, have been targeted for being sympathetic to the Oromo Liberation Army (an armed rebel group).

How do the affairs in Ethiopia, for example, affect the racial tensions in the U.S.? First of all, there is no civil unrest of this magnitude in the U.S. due to the civil rights movement that took place in the 1960s. There has been no such movement in any developed country in the world accentuated by China, for example, with its blatant record of human rights violations against the Tibetans, Uyghurs, and the citizens of Hong Kong and Taiwan. The U.S. Government and its people have created an *island* for themselves that keeps them separate from the rest of the world. According to Josefina, this CRT needs to be discussed from a global standpoint. It should be a matter that is brought to the attention of the United Nations. The slaughter of the Oromo people and other ethnic groups in Ethiopia is unacceptable. The tribal warfare in Ethiopia and other countries in Africa continue to this day, and it was the past conflicts of many of these groups that enslaved Africans and brought them to the western coast of their country to be sold to European merchants during the sixteenth and seventeenth centuries.

BIDEN'S CATASTROPHIC WITHDRAWAL FROM AFGHANISTAN

THE CRT IS not just an American concern. Why do American professors and politicians pin this issue solely on Americans? This is common because there is a strong magnetism to break down all problems in order to blame someone, either Whites or Blacks, Democrats or Republicans, slave owners or advocates for freemen. This lack of understanding race and other cultures is playing out in the Biden administration's decision to pull troops out of Afghanistan after a two-decade military campaign to defeat the Taliban. After reading some of Gilles Dorronsoro's article *The Winning Strategy in Afghanistan*, Rafael noted some important observations. There are more than 10,000 foreigners residing in Kabul who maintain a "distance" from the Afghan people and live a rich lifestyle in stark contrast to the native population of the capital. This smelled like CRT to Rafael, Josefina and their friends. Furthermore, instead of securing the population, the international community only protects its embassies and other key administration buildings. Half of the city is off-limits to Afghans creating serious traffics jams for the populace. The foreigners have huge salaries, and they often do not pay taxes. Neither do they learn the local language of the Afghans. All of this forges a deep suspicion among Afghans that the international coalition (IC) is secretly supporting the

Taliban. This becomes a propaganda tool the Taliban wisely uses to its advantage to convince the locals that the coalition is the enemy.

Adding to this cauldron of miscues, civilian casualties and arbitrary arrests from the IC have not only been exacerbating but alienating as well. There were more than 600 prisoners detained at the Bagram Air Base, and it was known that many were tortured and mistreated. Many of them were Afghan citizens, but Afghan laws did not apply to them because the IC didn't allow this to happen. Furthermore, the U.S. presence among the Pashtuns was very low. American soldiers have gone from being regarded as *mehman* (guest) to *dushman* (enemy). Again, the lack of understanding another culture and its ethnic diversity was the reason the U.S. and the coalition forces lost the battle in Afghanistan against the Taliban. The U.S. military needed to implement a better foreign language preparation plan in which its soldiers learned the local language of the community. The military personnel should have also lived among Afghans in order to establish friendly and cordial relationships with them. When in Rome, a person must live like the Romans. In other words, someone shouldn't isolate himself in wealthy enclaves and live a lifestyle of affluence in a country where most lack the basic necessities and live in extreme poverty. The U.S. can tout itself as having the best military in the world with the most advanced weapons, but if it lacks the "cultural arsenal," representative of the "heart" of any military investment, its enterprise is doomed to fail as it has done.

Another area of discontent among Afghans centered on the absence of integrity in managing international aid. There was poor coordination and accountability among the many subcontractors dispensing international aid, not taking into consideration the interests of the Afghans. This created a new Afghan elite that accumulated wealth during the war. Many of the "Uncultured-Upper Echelon" they were entitled to this aid, which has filled their pockets while little was used for infrastructure development and the basic needs of the vast majority of the population. All of this caused tension and jealousy among the locals, and the Taliban, as well as the "privileged," benefitted from foreign money and aid obtained through extortion. Some of the "crumbs" from this foreign investment fell through the cracks to the people who really needed the aid. Once again, the CRT played out among the Afghan *crème de la crème pigs* who discriminated against the poor and oppressed. The U.S. and other foreign powers seemed to lend a blind eye to this quandary, which further revealed the failed efforts of the IC to stabilize the country and end the fighting.

FRENCH AVARICE IS THE CULPRIT OF HAITI'S FAILED STATE

AS JOSEFINA AND Rafael contemplated the situation in Afghanistan, they received news of the assassination of Haiti's president, Jovenel Moïse, last Wednesday on July 7, 2021 at his residence on the outskirts of Port au Prince. He was a divisive leader, and many Haitians wanted him ousted. As most people know, Haiti is the poorest country in the Western Hemisphere. But the blame for Haiti's poverty and history of dictatorial rule by the Duvalier's, Papa and Baby Doc, falls on the shoulders of France. Haiti became a French colony in the seventeenth century, and at that time, France instituted slavery on the island by bringing African slaves there. During that time, Haiti became one of the richest colonies in the world due to its production of sugarcane. But in the late eighteenth century, the enslaved Blacks revolted and gained their independence. News of their independence never reached the slaves of the Southern United States because the American slaveholders did not want their slaves to develop any ideas of liberation. Haiti declared its independence from France in 1804, but in 1806, the country split with Alexandre Pétion ruling the south and Henry Christophe ruling the north. Rafael observed that this internal division could possibly be one of the factors explaining the centralized struggles Haiti has suffered from that time to the present.

Moreover, in 1814 King Louis XVIII wanted to see if he could get Haiti's rulers to surrender. Christophe appointed himself king of Haiti in 1811, and he refused to reinstate slavery on the island. However, Pétion wanted to negotiate and pay the French to have France honor Haiti's independence. He proposed to pay France 15 million francs as Napoléon did in 1803 when he sold Louisiana to the United States. Jean-Pierre Boyer became Pétion's successor when he died in 1818 and continued negotiations with France. Opposition from Christophe followed, but once he died in 1820, Boyer unified the two sides of the island. When Boyer tried to achieve suzerainty over Haiti, which would have established the island as a protectorate of France, Charles X, the successor of Louis XVIII, rebuked his proposal in 1824. But on April 17, 1825, Charles X decreed that France would honor Haiti's independence for a price of 150 million francs—ten times the amount paid by the U.S. for Louisiana. This amount was supposed to compensate for the French colonists' money lost during the post-slavery period. The king of France commissioned Baron de Mackau with his squadron of 14 brigs of war with more than 500 cannons to deliver the ordinance. If Boyer's administration rejected this offer, the French would have invaded Haiti. This was an egregious act of extortion not diplomacy.

Boyer had no choice but to sign this unfair document on July 11, 1825 due to the threat of imminent war. Haiti agreed to pay the sum of 150 million francs in five equal installments. There was no way the island could make these payments since the total was more than ten times its annual budget. Haiti had to borrow 30 million francs from French banks for the first two payments. No one was surprised when Haiti defaulted on these loans, but the new French King Louis Philippe I insisted the island comply on its commitment to pay by sending another expedition of 12 warships in 1838. In this revision deceptively labeled "Traité d'Amitié" (Treaty of Friendship), the French reduced the outstanding bill to 60 million francs. The Haitians had to take out outrageous loans to pay the balance. The French colonists claimed this amount totaling 90 million francs would only cover one-twelfth of the value of their lost properties, including slaves. The total was five times the annual budget of the French nation. Boyer incorporated draconian taxes to pay off the loans. Christopher had begun to build a national school system, but Boyer and all subsequent presidents after him put these types of projects on hold. Researchers have determined that this debt, which emptied the coffers of the Haitian treasury, resulted directly in underfunding the island's educational and healthcare systems along with the inability to develop its public infrastructure in the twentieth century. Current assessments confirm, that with all the interest earned from all the loans, the total amount was not paid in full until 1947, and Haiti ended up paying more than twice the value of the French colonists' claims of lost revenue. Thomas Piketty, a French economist, acknowledged that France should repay Haiti at least $28 billion U.S. dollars in restitution.

Numerous former French presidents—Jacques Chirac, Nicolas Sarkozy and François Hollande—have a history of ignoring Haiti's demands for compensation. Hollande, France's second head of state to ever visit Haiti, arrived on the island in May, 2015. At the time he stated France should address the discreditable debt.. When he realized the issue ignited the legal fuel already prepared in the "coals" by Attorney Ira Kurzban on behalf of the Haitians, Hollande corrected himself by underlying that he meant France's debt was only a "moral" one. Jean-Bertrand Aristide, the former Haitian president, had pleaded for a total recompense in 2002. The debt to Haiti is not isolated to this island since the French eventually abolished slavery in its colonies of Martinique, Guadeloupe, Réunion and French Guyana in 1848, although they remain as French territories in the present. The French also compensated the former owners of slaves in these countries. All of this resulted in the racial wealth gap. In France 14.1 percent of the French live below the poverty line. In Martinique and Guadeloupe (more that 80 percent of the population is of African descent), the poverty rates are 38-46 percent, but among Haitians the rate is at 59 percent. The median annual income of a French family is $31,112 while for a Haitian family it's $450. There is no doubt Haiti should be at the center of the world's concern for reparations due to the economic sabotage of Afro-Haitians and their descendants by the grossly unjust indemnity Haiti paid France. What's absurd is that it is the first and only time a formerly enslaved colony was forced to pay those who once enslaved them.

As Rafael and Josefina enjoyed watching the beautiful and historical sites along the countryside of France during the 2021 Tour de France, it was difficult not to think about the hypocrisy of the French who stole the wealth from countries like Haiti and the other Caribbean islands to enrich themselves. While Haiti struggles with the current assassination of its president along with the instability of the island's political, economic and social entities, France basks in the sun from the extortion and spoils it gained during its infamous period of slavery. As the riders finish their finale on the Champs-Élysées, the millions of dollars paid to the riders and their sponsors along with the money earned by presenting this event to the world through the lens of the media and television represent the unfathomable avarice of the French, who have feasted off of the platter of racism and exploitation of Africans and their descendants, in countries like Haiti. What would God say about this? What does the mammoth Arc de Triomphe in Paris really symbolize when it was inaugurated in 1836 by the French King Louis-Philippe? It is clear it is a symbol of France's racist attack and rape of its African neighbors.

AMERICA'S BROTHEL HOUSE IN CUBA

ANOTHER TOPIC THAT interested Rafael and his bicycle companion Ramón was the recent protests in Cuba against the new President Miguel Díaz-Canel who replaced the elder Raúl Castro. The U.S. embargo along with the Covid-19 crisis and the volatility of Venezuela was really affecting the Cuban people since they received much of their food supply and oil from Venezuela. In addition, tourism to the island has declined due the world pandemic, and the former Trump administration closed the Western Union locations there where Cubans would receive money from friends and relatives abroad. It's important to mention the dictatorship of Fulgencio Batista who basically ruled Cuba with the support of the U.S. from 1952 until 1959 when he was overthrown by Fidel Castro. Batista's reign centered on the brutal repression of any dissident and the total corruption of his administration aided by the influence of the U.S. and the presence of the Mafia. Cuba became the brothel of America.

Batista grew up in a simple home, the son of two Mestizo peasants. He grew up cutting sugarcane and later enlisted in the army. He had many friends, he enjoyed the gift of gab, and he was a womanizer. Batista was also a bibliophile who read everything that fell into his hands. With time he made a name for himself in the military, political environment, judiciary circles and among students. This background served him well when the population disapproved of the dictatorship of Gerardo Machado, a Liberal who became repressive. Batista came to power after the *Rebelión de los Sargentos* (Rebellion of the Sergeants). The U.S., which had an influence in Cuba since the war with Spain in 1898, viewed him as an ambitious and favorable figurehead because he aligned himself with the politics of the Good Neighbor Policy of 1933 established by Franklin Delano Roosevelt. This policy emphasized trade and cooperation instead of military intervention between the U.S. and the countries of Central and Latin America, which contrasted with the isolationist stance of previous U.S. administrations.

Batista took advantage of his affable position when the populace was very discontent when the repressive rule of Machado ended in 1933, and Carlos Manuel de Céspedes became the provisional president. But Céspedes formed a weak government that could not satisfy Cuban society. He was soon replaced by Ramón Grau San Martín. The Good Neighbor Policy benefited the U.S. and Cuba under the new leadership. Cuba was able to profit more from the exportation of sugar, special agricultural privileges, energy, banking and the convenience of the U.S. Guantánamo Bay Naval Base in the southeastern region of the island. These mutual interests were met when Batista deposed of President San Martín, who was too far to the Left, and placed Carlos Mendieta in command because he was more favorable to the White House policies. Mendieta took the peasants out of the large plantations, ordered the assassination of Marxists leaders, allowed the U.S. to regain control of the electrical company and rented the Guantánamo base to the American-military administration indefinitely.

Furthermore, Mendieta, as Batista's political puppet, repealed the Platt Amendment (which gave the U.S. the right to invade the island militarily), created an amnesty for political leaders, legalized the Communist Party and enacted economic reforms to improve the impoverished lives of the local community. Because of these favorable conditions, Batista successfully gained the presidency of Cuba in 1940. During the end of his presidency in 1944, the social restlessness rose again. Scrupulously, he accepted his former adversary San Martín to succeed him. Batista relocated to Daytona Beach, Florida where he reunited with Meyer Lansky, an old business associate, who happened to be a Mafia boss in Miami. This relationship established a gateway for capital and killers from the North American Mafia families to reach Cuba. In 1946 the peak of the Mafia imprint in Havana with a plethora of criminals was evident with the likes of Lucky Luciano, Vito Genovese, Santo Trafficante, Jr., Albert Anastasia and Frank Costello. They would often socialize in the National Hotel of the island due to their friendship with Batista. Shortly thereafter, Batista returned to Cuba and overthrew President Carlos Prío Socarrás with the backing of the Cuban military in 1952. Corruption now ruled his presidency with the prevalence of luxurious hotels and casinos, and he silenced his opposition by censorship, jail, torture and executions. His reign ended when Fidel Castro and his *guerrilleros* triumphantly defeated Batista and forced him, his brother and Lansky to leave the island on December 31, 1958. Batista fled to the Dominican Republic and Portugal before settling in Spain where he died in 1973.

Josefina also acknowledged the U.S. Government controlled the Cuban economy during this period, and this caused a lot of resentment among the Cuban people. In the late 1950s, U.S. companies owned 90 percent of Cuban mines, 80 percent of its public utilities, 50 percent of its railroad infrastructure, 40 percent of its sugar production and 25 percent of its bank deposits, about $1 billion in total. Political leaders under the Batista regime along with many American miscreants enriched themselves at the expense of the general population who lived in degraded conditions. The American multinational International Telephone and Telegraph Corporation (ITT) presented Batista with a golden phone for allowing the exorbitant telephone rate increases, which overfilled the pockets of the Americans and Batista cohorts. Most of the aid Cuba received from the U.S. was in the form of weapons assistance, which only strengthened the military of the Batista dictatorship. Until the overthrow of the Cuban dictator by Castro, the American Ambassador Earl E. T. Smith was just as influential as Batista, if not more so.

It's easy to understand why Fidel Castro gained the support of the people and was able to topple the Batista regime. Furthermore, one can earnestly empathize with the Cubans who endured the exploitation of the U.S. Government and Batista's rule. Rafael realized the Biden administration today is incapable of viewing the history of this island from a lens that accepts responsibility for the injustices the U.S. unwitting and ignorantly facilitated in begetting in Cuba. It is also logical that many Cubans looked to Marxism as their salvation where the same social class would be established for all. This would be the only fair and legitimate solution to the ills fomented by the U.S. The Batista dictatorship and the U.S. basically reinstituted a new form of twentieth century "slavery" by using the Cuban people to work in the fields and mines for low wages while the *HAUGHTY* elite, Mafia, U.S. personnel and foreigners gambled in the luxurious hotels and casinos and fornicated with Cuban prostitutes in the brothels. Cuba became one "Big Whore House" for Americans and other wealthy tourists from around the world.

The Biden administration must begin the dialogue with the current Cuban President Miguel Díaz-Canel now that Fidel Castro is dead, and his brother Raúl is no longer the chief commander. The main weakness the U.S. has demonstrated since Fidel took power in 1959 is that it basically does not speak Spanish. The English only attitude or so called language of "diplomacy" is a reminder of the American imperialistic and imbecilic vestiges in Cuba and other countries in Central and Latin America. The Spanish Empire forced their language on the Indigenous tribes of the New World when they conquered these lands in the fifteenth century. The U.S. would demonstrate their respect for the culture and heritage of Cuba by learning Spanish. Then, it might be possible to discuss easing up on the stifling sanctions the U.S. has imposed on Cuba since Castro had been in power. But Cuba would have to concede something in return. Maybe they could allow citizens to apply for dual citizenship with the U.S. in order to travel freely from the U.S. to Cuba. This might help open the door for more economic opportunities for the Cuban people who have been oppressed for so long.

DEBT, EXCESSIVE PROCREATION AND INDECISION ARE RUINOUS

AS JOSEFINA AND Rafael continued to discuss political problems abroad, they realized that education, health and the ability to manage financial issues are key. Education prepares a person for the career he chooses, and this obviously is necessary for earning a living. But an individual many times gets stuck when he is more concerned about how much money he can make. He often forgets to prioritize his health and essential necessities. As long as he has enough money to feed, clothe and house himself, he has everything he needs at the time. Saving is the fundamental value he like most people ignore. This insatiable desire to buy the biggest home possible, the most luxurious car available and a vacation home somewhere exotic to fill his materialistic appetite consumes him. He doesn't have a problem with going into debt to obtain these things. Additionally, he ignores his health because he is too preoccupied with working and paying mortgages and other payments from month to month. It's a cycle that becomes more entrenched as the years go by.

Why are these concepts so difficult for countries in Central and Latin America where the discrepancy between the very wealthy and poor is so pronounced? One of the main reasons for the prevalence of poverty in these countries is the large families that many Hispanics have. It is part of their culture and tradition, fomented by the Catholic Church, to procreate and have many children. Obviously, it becomes difficult for parents making a minimum wage to consider how to save money when they are trying just to feed themselves and their children from day to day. There should be a cultural shift encouraged by the Church to encourage families to wait before having children. Birth control education should be offered to young couples to help them understand the significance of financial security for themselves and their families. Churches, schools and other government agencies should teach the general population, especially the poor, about the significance of managing their money. In Third World countries, these types of institutions may not exist due to the lack of infrastructure, but there is no excuse for the Church not to take the lead in informing people about this in their weekly Masses. God would want all of us to enjoy the benefits of having enough money to sustain ourselves.

Enrique, one of Rafael's friends, reminded him of another aspect of education people often forget or discount as nonsense. Johann Wolfgang von Goethe, the renowned German poet, playwright and novelist, advocated for each man to know and believe in himself. By learning about great thinkers like Goethe, a person becomes familiar with his Western heritage, and cultural statesmen like Goethe can be role models for society. From his well-known *Faust*, he writes: "Lose this day loitering—'twill be the same story tomorrow and the next more dilatory… Each indecision brings its own delays, and days are lost lamenting o'er lost days." Indecision can paralyze someone when he procrastinates and does not make a decision to act on something. People often put off saving until later in life, or they fail to obtain a college degree until the right moment. Goethe reminds each person "delaying" becomes a habit that hamstrings him in his pursuits. Goethe goes on to say: "Seize this very minute—Boldness has genius, power and magic in it. Only engage, and then the mind grows heated—Begin it, and then the work will be completed!" In his lifetime that spanned 82 years, his literary work is encased in 133 huge volumes. His masterpiece *Faust* is considered one of the major works of modern literature.

Rafael and Josefina thought often thought about Goethe's wise comments as they sat together watching the Tokyo 2020 Olympics over the past few weeks. They observed the heroic fearlessness of the athletes competing on the most important world stage for many of them. There were always those who fulfilled their ultimate dreams of winning a medal and those who achieved their goals of doing their best. Some followed the process learned in their training while others focused on the end result without trusting the process. The U.S. 4x100-meter men's team finished a dismal sixth place in one of their semifinal races on the track not qualifying for the final heat. This was the first time the U.S. had not advanced for this event in numerous years. There was an issue with lost time in the exchange of the baton during the second leg of the relay from which they were not able to recover. The athletes and media focused on their failure.

Sometimes the process works and other times it does not. But the central question should be: "Did those American athletes act and run with a relentless and zestful boldness?" There is a fine line between victory and defeat, which should not be exclusively defined by success or failure but by the intention and decision of an athlete doing his best in any given moment. This becomes the elusive yardstick that eludes many people because winning is so intoxicating they forget the value of losing. Losing can be enlightening as well as long as a person remembers the victor and defeated are synonymous in the pursuit of the Olympic dream. At times he will win, and there are other times he will lose. But by focusing on losing only, he ties his hands and paralyzes himself from trying. Goethe reminds the athlete not to spend his time loitering but to spend it engaged for the "next race." Loitering will generate future failures while engagement will lead to success because it is the final result of a *dauntlessness* intention. Nobody ever won a race by "sauntering" because to begin with, he never would have toed the starting line.

TREASURING ENTHUSIASM AND SOLITUDE

THE OLYMPICS ALSO gives man the opportunity to appreciate enthusiasm. This emotion is born in the soul not the physical body. Henry Wadsworth Longfellow (1807-1882), an American poet, wrote the poem "A Psalm of Life." He writes: "Tell me not, in mournful numbers, Life is but an empty dream!—For the soul is dead that slumbers, And things are not what they seem." When a person only considers life from the perspective of the body aging and dying, he allows his anima "to slumber." There is no doubt that the body will die and return to dust, but the soul lives on with God. Rafael realized that this understanding of the noumenon is very difficult to foster and nurture throughout life. The enthusiasm for life comes from the soul and nowhere else. Longfellow goes on to say: "Life is real! Life is earnest! And the grave is not its goal; Dust thou art, to dust returnest, Was not spoken of the soul." Man's soul resides within his body, and he must take care of the body knowing eventually it will decay. But as an individual sits in medical offices throughout the world waiting to see a doctor to monitor his health, he should take a moment to breathe in deeply and touch his soul. The happy spirit is the one that laughs regardless of his circumstances. Knowing and believing his soul "*lives*" is the main purpose of his life, one that he must strive to acknowledge and conduct his life according to this understanding.

As a writer, Rafael cherished the time he spent in solitude to hear and feel his soul. This was an essential part required for balancing his life. When he became absorbed in the busyness of living, he yearned for time to be alone. Most people can't stand being away from others because the distraction from self is common. It is what society inherently teaches everyone. Rafael, Josefina and their friends supposed that in modern-day society people feel the need to be engaged each moment of the day in some sort of activity or with someone else. Unfortunately, many resort to suicide as the answer when they can't come to terms with being comfortable being alone, part of the time. In solitude a person is forced to come face to face with his inner self.. By acknowledging this truth, he is forced to dialogue with God. God wants each person to seek him in prayer and silence. The journey of the poet like Longfellow or any person, who chooses to write, becomes the source for exploring his human desire to be whole and enthusiastic about this brief existence he and everyone lives. Man goes from point A (birth) to point B (death). If he disregards this reality, he will live life without meaning. If he comes to the realization that "yes" the body dies and turns to dust, but the soul lives on, he can live with purpose, meaning and enthusiasm.

What's difficult for human beings to comprehend and wrap their minds around is when they are alone, they don't always hear a mortal voice talking to them. Being still requires great effort and concentration. It involves feeling uncomfortable, and it may seem unproductive. An individual's thoughts slow down when he sits in quietude. The process of "decelerating" allows him to observe the mindlessness of the many things he does. Rafael and Josefina were reminded of Carla, a close friend. Carla had been divorced four times, and now she was in a new relationship with someone who lived in another state. She had recently retired and had the time to travel back and forth from San Antonio to Milwaukee. Carla tried to retain her friendship with her girlfriends when she was in town. But most of time, the gatherings had to be on her terms because she was busy doing one chore after another. In the latest social gathering, they were going to get together for dinner, but Carla stated she had already eaten; therefore, she could come but wouldn't eat. Being around Carla with her need to find another man and stay busy all the time was obvious. Rafael, many times, concluded it was best to remove himself from this type of *alliance* because it was, in his mind, superficial and toxically virulent. He didn't want to be the object of her busyness. In her need to be occupied, she is oblivious of how she treats others like "ping pong balls" to be tossed around to satisfy her ego's appetite, importance and entertainment.

THE MIRRORED FAILURE OF VIETNAM IN AFGHANISTAN

AFTER THINKING ABOUT personal relationships, Rafael's attention shifted back to focusing and listening to the latest development in national news and reading about the withdrawal of American troops from Afghanistan. This incited him to begin doing some research to understand the failure of the war there. It was similar to the defeat of the Vietnam War. The Americans believed they could win the war in both of these countries through attrition. Having superior technology and weaponry, the U.S. thought they could wear the Taliban and Vietcong down, and the latter two would eventually surrender because they would lose the will to continue fighting. In addition, the U.S. was under the impression that if they helped Afghans establish a democracy from a national point of view, focusing on the urban centers like Kabul, this form of government would expand to the communities in the rural areas. They ignored the clans, leaders and elders of these rural outposts who would have been able to gain the confidence and respect of the Afghan people. Most Afghans knew the government in Kabul along with the police force throughout the country were corrupt. Instead of knocking down doors and searching for guerrilla fighters in the urban, as well as the rural areas, the coalition forces should have concentrated their efforts on protecting the lives of the civilians and building schools, hospitals and other important infrastructure. The U.S. should have dedicated 90 percent of their time to politics and nation building and 10 percent to warfare.

If the U.S. would have taken the twenty-year war in Afghanistan more seriously, they should have sent more District Reconstruction Teams (DRTs). These teams rely on the U.S. State Department to send more officers to Afghanistan. There are at the present time more Foreign Service Officers (FSOs) in Rome than there are in southern and eastern Afghanistan. There were hundreds of FSOs deployed to Vietnam, which was a good thing. There are less than twenty today in southern Afghanistan. It was recommended that 600-800 Pashto-speaking FSOs from the U.S. Agency for International Development should have been distributed among the 200 district-reconstruction teams, and this could have really made a significant impact in defeating the Taliban. During the first eight years since the start of Operation Enduring Freedom, only thirteen FSOs were trained to learn Pashto, and only two of them were in Afghanistan. This really explains why the U.S. has failed in Afghanistan because the military mindset is to enter, find and destroy. This "Rambo" military style ignores the intellectual and cultural muscle necessary to be successful in a country like Afghanistan. The Pashto language, in this case, becomes the weapon to penetrate and cohabitate with the civilians and the real leaders who will be respected by their people. The U.S. still lives in the Dark Ages when it comes to stretching its monolingual mind to extending and operating in a world beyond America's borders where others speak a foreign language, incomprehensible to the feeble-minded American who flexes his biceps at the expense of his "pencil neck" brain.

Rafael and Josefina continued to think about the Taliban regaining control of the provinces throughout Afghanistan as its intention of capturing Kabul became apparent. Their thoughts returned to the Vietnam War. Josefina had just finished reading the article "How Not to 'Win Hearts and Minds'" by George C. Herring (2017). Herring states that at the beginning of the Vietnam War, the intentions of

American officials were to win the hearts and minds (WHAM) of the South Vietnamese people. They regarded this to be the key to victory. Unfortunately, the Americans were doomed to fail because they were not equipped linguistically and culturally to lead a successful campaign. It was Bui Diem, South Vietnam's ambassador to Washington from 1965 to 1972, who noted that the two countries were quite different and apart. Very few of the Americans sent to South Vietnam had a basic understanding of the language and its history. Neither were they familiar with Vietnam's religious traditions, cultural etiquettes or politics. The goal of the war for the Americans was to uphold their credibility as a superpower in the world whereas the South Vietnamese fought for its existence.

Furthermore, the U.S. did not establish a combined command structure with the South Vietnamese as it did in Korea. The Republic of Vietnam was demeaned when the U.S. required it to take on the role of pacification. The Americans created an ambience of dependency in a country that sought its independence. Naturally, tensions between the two cultures became worse. The intruders looked down on the Vietnamese; like in Kabul, the opulent lifestyle of the Americans contrasted with the poverty of the locals. Americans built enormous bases equipped with air conditioning, shopping centers and movie theaters. Many of the troops sped their trucks and cars through traffic at excessive speeds endangering the lives of the locals. Prostitution became a serious problem as well.

The U.S. forces in Vietnam basically "prostituted" the young women physically and also debauched the country as a whole with their ignorance and cavalier approach towards the people of this Asian country. It was appalling to Rafael and his friends to think about the type of terrorism the Americans administered in the Vietnam and Afghanistan Wars. In Vietnam there were approximately 58,220 American soldier casualties compared to 2,000,000 civilians in North and South Vietnam, 1,100,000 North Vietnamese and Vietcong fighters and between 200,000-250,000 South Vietnamese soldiers. In

Afghanistan, approximately 69,000 Afghan Security Forces, 51,000 civilians and about 51,000 Taliban militants have died. The coalition forces suffered the loss of 3,500 soldiers, two-thirds of whom were Americans, with 20,000 U.S. soldiers wounded since the war began in 2001. During the September 11th terrorist attack of 2001 in New York, 2,977 civilians, primarily Americans, were killed when two planes collided into the twin towers. These numbers demonstrate a disproportionate amount of deaths among foreigners killed in the Vietnam and Afghanistan conflicts in comparison to Americans who perished in these tragic events.

Terrorism becomes a relative term depending on where a person lives in the world and what his perspective is. How could the Vietnamese and people of Afghanistan not view the endless bombing of their countries by Americans and other coalition forces as a form of terrorism of the worst kind? Americans tend to see only one side of the coin, which is their viewpoint only. What's interesting is the enemy in these two wars lost more civilians and soldiers but still won the war. Watching the news last night on August 16, 2021 with the Taliban overtaking Kabul and a U.S. cargo plane surrounded by Afghan civilians mobbing the runway with people clinging to the wings and trying to climb aboard was reminiscent of the abandonment of U.S. forces and American civilians in Saigon in 1975, when the Vietcong and North Vietnamese had overtaken South Vietnam. South Vietnamese civilians hung on to American helicopters and drowned in the South China Sea as the U.S. soldiers left them defenseless in their wake. The only thing President Biden said last night was that Afghan Security Forces did not have the will to fight the Taliban. Mr. Biden, 69,000 Afghan Security Forces have been killed since the war began in 2001 compared to approximately 2,333 American soldiers. How could the president of the U.S. state such an erroneous and flagrant statement?

PEDAL STROKES ON RURAL ROADS

RAFAEL AND RAMÓN rode their road bikes for a 50-mile trek out towards Seguin from Cibolo, Texas. They turned on Settler's Road, a rural road about 20 miles from Cibolo. The fine gravel from Rafael's accident just shy of two years still remained there as if untouched. It was a metaphorical reminder of the balancing act someone faces in life from a personal and global perspective. Rafael remembered the swelling in his left cheek after the initial surgery two months when two titanium metal plates were placed in his upper cheek area to repair two small bones in the zygomatic cavity. He recalled sitting in the reclining chair in the office waiting for the doctors to alleviate the infection bubbling in the surgical location, which had been healing nicely for two months. The doctor injected a needle with local anesthesia in three different areas above the left side of the upper teeth. After a few minutes, another doctor arrived and proceeded to open Rafael's mouth wide as he cut into the skin of the upper gum area with his scrapple. Rafael braced himself by holding the armrests on each side of the chair. He also moaned as they dug in a little further. Sensing the discomfort and pain, the doctors administered another injection on the outside of his left cheek. He saw the needle coming towards him in slow motion as he grimaced some more. Then, they proceeded to insert a small straw-like piece of plastic to drain the pus that had accumulated in the area. They also applied more pressure on the infected site to drain the pus. Finally, they added one or two stitches to keep the plastic piece in place.

Rafael and Ramón talked about many things as they crossed the notorious crossroad now dormant in Rafael's unconscious mind. They chatted about family, politics and racing; words flowed easily as they pedaled along enduring the asphalt's heat and humidity of this summer day in August. Life is much like a pedal stroke that continually revolves like pages turning in a book by its reader. It was like another sentence in the paragraph of a chapter or like another breath in a person's life. It was the stream of consciousness of one life lived and shared with another. The wind warmed their bodies as the caked sunscreen on their faces, legs and arms absorbed the sweat creating a quagmire of dirt, grime, dead gnats and thick white cream. Their tongues greeted the warm electrolytes carried in their water bottles with a resigned delight. It did quench their thirst temporarily as they imagined the cool drink later at Subway with chilling-cold ice bouncing from the dispenser into cups, which would be their reward.

CONSTABLE'S CANVAS AND TWO WHITE CATS

RAFAEL'S ATTENTION TURNED to John Constable (1776-1837), an English artist born in East Bergholt, Suffolk. He was not a renowned painter, but he is known for his portraits of the idyllic country life in England. He was concerned with portraying ideas about morality and intellectual truth. It is interesting to know he did not travel abroad nor did he go outside of England. Constable met and eventually married Maria Bicknell. Since he was not able to earn a decent salary as an artist at the time, he waited for the death of his parents, which provided him a legacy and an assured income. John and Maria married in London in 1816. They had seven children together, but in 1828 Maria died of tuberculosis. Constable was devastated by her passing.

Salisbury Cathedral from the South West (1811) stood out to Rafael. This piece depicts the steeple of the cathedral blending in nicely with the grey and white clouds in the blue sky with the dark green leaves blending in with the abbey and steeple. It's almost as if the church is growing out of the earth and trees. The brown hues of the church building and the spiraling conifer of its elongated structure match the brown strokes of color in the white clouds just above it. The closeness of the cathedral to the viewer reveals the artist is nearby, almost immersed in Nature, establishing a union between man, Nature and architecture. In the foreground it's imperceptible, but the admirer can distinguish some tiny red-motored vehicles of the day almost disappearing in the green grass and road in front of the building. It almost appears to resemble ants moving and working tirelessly. There is no doubt it was an approach the Impressionists later developed in the nineteenth century. This same painting was exhibited in the Royal Academy of England in 1823, but it was a glossy and very finished work, which appealed to popular taste.

The "intellectual truth" in this raw and nature-like painting suggests that Constable, as the artist, seeks to pierce into the heavens with his paintbrush almost as if to awaken man from his separateness from himself, others, Nature and God. The brownish and grey clouds directly above the steeple seem to capture its reflection and appears to stain the white-colossal embodiments with its hue. The combination of colors and oil provide a view without a clear picture, almost like a mirage from a good distance away. In Rafael's mind it was almost as if he could see God, but the Divine is distilled in the image of Nature in front of Rafael. It generates a certain type of silence after a period of hard work or physical activity. Rafael felt that "miraculous silence" today after participating in a sprint triathlon early this morning in his neighborhood of Alamo Heights. He and Josefina, along with about 298 participants, swam 400 meters in the 50-meter pool about one mile from their home. They circled around a 3-mile loop on bike along the long-standing dam of this iconic race named Dam 09, referencing the last two-numerical digits of their area code, to finish with a 2.5 mile run along the adjacent-cemented trail of a set of soccer fields and grassy park. When they returned home, after visiting with friends and other competitors, there was such a sense of peace and tranquility permeating within. Their small cottage like home with deep-white-colored plantation shutters filtered the bright light fanning into its interior solitude. Stunning reflections bounced off of the stain-glassed window wall at the end of the kitchen leading to the sun and dining room where another large stained-glassed-paned fenestella dripped its red, yellow and green colors into the lush backyard. There were two white kittens, Rico and Nola, resting in their usual places—one under the gas grill and the other under the table under a large oak tree in the back corner of their secluded paradise. Time was stilled for the moment when the activity of the triathlon and the rituals of gathering the needed equipment (bike, helmet, running shoes and swim googles) all vanished like the early morning darkness of dusk at 6 am when Rafael and Josefina pedaled softly to the pool through the quiet streets with their flickering red and white lights on their bikes.

The image of the newspaper was displayed on the wood table in the sunroom along with the empty box of tennis balls laying by the Mexican ceramic pot with the tall plant. Two kittens playing hide and seek in the cardboard box highlighted God's presence in the midst of a simple pleasure of watching them play. The sweetness of a nap after a cleansing shower on the soft sheets with a rhythmic fan blowing overhead felt good on the skin. Looking through the leaflets of the shutter, Rafael could see the tall grass that needed cutting. The dried up blossoms of African-like plants in front were resting where the humming bird from yesterday drank. The quietness was counterbalanced by the humidity and soft breeze swaying in the branches across the street. The arched structure painted in white of the front-porch entrance of the grey house could be seen at a bird's eye view. The reduced amount of traffic crossing at this slow hour of a Saturday afternoon in the midst of August reminds a person of the steady hand of God's presence in his life. There was a certain "morality" experienced at the hand of the artist with his paintbrush or keyboard stroking away. The separation between letters and words was nonexistent at this juncture of placidity where the hum of the cool air escaping from the vent above resonated.

THE U.S. LOSES ITS GLOBAL CREDIBILITY AS A BEACON OF DEMOCRACY

RAFAEL'S ATTENTION TURNED again to the plight of Afghanistan and the mistake the U.S. and allied forces made. It seems like they underestimated the ability of the Taliban to gain the support of the elders and warlords from the provinces surrounding Kabul. The Taliban is a mixture of al-Qaida, ISIS and a diaspora of other fighters who could be bribed to join their groups to fight against the Afghan Security Forces. For one the Taliban spoke the native Pashto and other dialects of Afghanistan because obviously they were fighting in their endemic nation. They also inherently knew politics in their native country had always been historically decentralized. Most realized President Ashraf Ghani was a puppet set up by the U.S. and coalition forces. Instead of viewing the problem in Afghanistan from the inside looking in, the U.S. and its allies were surveying the complexity of this foreign land from the outside in. The Taliban is the culmination of the elder leaders from the provinces who defeated the British during their colonial period, the Russians in the 1980s and now the fall of the U.S. after their involvement in 2001.

The U.S. failed because it never had a clearly defined purpose in Afghanistan just like it floundered to construct one in Vietnam in the 1970s. The U.S. should have learned from Vietnam that the North

Vietnamese were fighting a civil war against South Vietnam. There was no fear the communist ideals propagated by North Vietnam would disseminate to the rest of the world as the U.S. suspected. The U.S. again misunderstood the cultural grassroots of the war in Vietnam. When someone is unfamiliar with the language and culture of Vietnam, he can never truly comprehend the conflict at hand. The situation in Afghanistan represents the victory by the Taliban for itself and all terrorist groups around the world who want to harm and destroy the influence of the U.S., western countries and other democratic nations around the globe. The imbroglio for the U.S. becomes its inability to see beyond its own cultural foundation built on capitalism, democracy and the monolingual approach of English only when confronted with events affecting the rest of the world. Unfortunately, the U.S. will continue to become a diminished player in foreign affairs as countries like Russia, China and Iran gain an upper hand in Asia and the Middle East. Americans are too comfortable living in a country of relative peace that does not and will never recognize the nuances of war that have plagued countries like Vietnam and Afghanistan for the major part of their history.

Furthermore, the mask debacle, resulting from the COVID-19 pandemic and its delta variant, has become a political battleground between Republicans and Democrats. It's an existential fiasco that Americans can't overcome as they claim liberty is at stake when Washington under Biden attempts to mandate a law requiring all people to wear masks and get vaccinated to safeguard themselves from the virus. Americans, for the most part, can't see past the "mask debate" that divides them, much like the maxim stating, "A family divided against itself" will fall. Americans only sympathize with one side of the mask debate, and it only pertains to the components affecting them. Likewise, the U.S. quickly forgets the horrific number of deaths in Afghanistan where 100,000 Afghan civilians and 50,000 Afghan soldiers have died in comparison to approximately 2,000 American soldiers. American and coalition forces were beginning to have an impact there with women attending school and gaining jobs in the press, politics and many other sectors. But Americans could not withstand the thought it was going to take longer than a 20-year involvement. To penetrate this civilization and gain the respect of the provinces, the U.S. presence along with the coalition allies needed to remain there indefinitely working together with the Afghan people and the Taliban, for that matter, to continue making progress and adapting to their ways of government not ours. Americans as a whole never understood Afghanistan and never will because of their innate inability and lack of interest to learn about the Middle East and other countries in the Third World like Africa and Latin America. This deficiency in cultural planning for America's futuristic role in the world is a grim one because most Americans live in a closed "closet" where money and profit are the name of the game, regardless of what is happening in the rest of the global playground.

Americans are only awakened temporarily when they were attacked like they were on September 11, 2001, but when these attacks occur, they do not prepare to confront the existential threat from ignoring others culturally and intellectually. Yesterday, on August 26, 2021, an ISIS-suicide bomber killed 15 American soldiers and around 169 Afghan civilians crowded on the outside wall of the Kabul airport. This was expected to happen since Biden has cowered to the Taliban's advance, an American mistake of epic proportions. When the U.S. military stopped working with the Afghan Army, the Taliban overtook the country in a matter of weeks. Even though the world and President Biden observed the takeover by the Taliban, he did nothing to halt the course of the insurgents. Biden did not want to commit more U.S. forces to stop the progression of the enemy. He even chose to close down Bagram Air Base, the largest U.S. airfield in Afghanistan that was well protected with a large perimeter around it to protect military personnel. The U.S. should have at least kept this airbase open to assist in the evacuation of Americans, coalition troops and Afghans who have assisted the Americans as interpreters and in other capacities. The most surprising and shocking revelation became evident when Biden's team started negotiating with the Taliban to give the U.S. time to evacuate. It was completely ludicrous to watch Biden and the "woke" officials in his cabinet conferring with the enemy they've been battling for 20 years. It doesn't take a war general to realize this fatal mistake. There was no doubt Biden should have been impeached or court marshalled immediately.

But when Rafael and Josefina probed deeper into the background of Biden and the many politicians and military staff under his administration, it becomes obvious Biden is not culturally or intellectually prepared to deal with the complex issues of Afghanistan, Pakistan, Russia, China and the rest of the world outside of the U.S. He tries to portray himself with his squinting eyes as a "Clint Eastwood spaghetti-western-tough guy" who stares down the enemy with his macho expression and pointed finger. Biden, in his arrogance as a leader of the U.S. and in his hesitant language and English only dialect, cannot possibly penetrate the political complexities of foreign countries because he has no experience living abroad. His isolation of growing up in Pennsylvania prepared him for a political office in that state and within the confinement of the U.S. only. In today's world it is essential to travel during an individual's formative years as he receives a high school and college education, and it's a prerequisite to live abroad, whether in Europe or any other part of the world outside of the U.S. It becomes imperative to learn and become fluent in at least one other language besides English. Trying to come across as a compassionate president does the complete opposite when he doesn't speak another language. Knowing some Pashto would have given Biden a compassionate advantage in comprehending the progress made for Afghan women and girls being allowed to go to school and work outside of the home. Without that ability to speak directly to the people in their own language, the U.S. and Biden, especially, have failed to truly commit to helping that country achieve the political goals they were beginning to attain with the assistance of the international coalition.

Assuming the position of totaling withdrawing from Afghanistan is so lame and harming because it now endangers India, Israel and other countries in the Middle East and the rest of the world. The Afghan people were beginning to see the excesses and failures of extremist groups like al-Qaida, ISIS and the Taliban. This cultural awakening of the possibilities beyond the strict rules of these terrorists was beginning to take shape in Afghanistan. It's a process for which Biden and the majority of the U.S. population lacked the patience to fulfill. A cultural and intellectual transformation of a country takes decades upon decades to achieve. It's not like taking four semesters of Spanish or Pashto, as part of a person's college degree plan; then, after passing those courses, he assumes he is finished learning the language and about the culture where that language is spoken. Rafael, as a former Spanish and French teacher, remembered asking the basic American college graduate who took some language courses: *"¿Cómo te llamas?* or *Comment tu t'appelles?"* (What is your name?) Nine out of ten students would respond: "Whoa, whoa, that was a long time ago! What does that mean?" This lack of knowing a foreign language translates into a mentality of vulnerability where Americans insulate themselves from the rest of the world; when they venture out into a foreign land, they often say, "Do you speak English?" This is the ultimate insult to members of another country outside of the U.S. or England. Until this mindset changes, the U.S. will continue to make epic international blunders like the one witnessed in Vietnam and most recently in Afghanistan. The world is in the most dangerous position it has ever been in due to the ignorance of Biden and his administration.

The balance of power is shifting in favor of rogue nations like Russia, China, North Korea and Iran. The U.S. military as well as the other coalition forces have an obligation to other countries like Afghanistan. The 9/11 attack on U.S. soil marked the beginning of a new world war where the enemy can't be seen, but it is known that he trains, recruits and operates in unstable and lawless countries like Afghanistan and Pakistan. Rafael recalled a statement made by a former marine who stated that military personnel does not train to stay in place along the shorelines of the U.S. with binoculars to see if the enemy is approaching by sea or air. But it is meant to be engaged culturally and militarily with other countries. Afghanistan was beginning to experience stability, and this is why the Taliban and the U.S. began to have conversations in regards to a cease-fire and other agreements. This does not mean U.S. military advisors and politicians should start to trust the Taliban, but they should mediate from a position of power. But when you begin to withdraw apologetically, the Taliban starts to reintroduce its tactics of taking away the rights of women and reinstating public executions. By granting the Taliban complete and unrestrained access to enter and control Kabul before the Americans and other Afghans, who cooperated with the U.S. military intelligence community, exit the country, the U.S. commanders are arbitrating from a position of profound weakness.

The whole idea of ending the war in Afghanistan was erroneous. The war will never end, and this is something the American psyche cannot grasp. A constant presence of the American military and coalition forces must remain there indefinitely to continually assist the Afghan military and citizens who want a free and brighter future. There were no American casualties during the last 18 months with the reduced forces narrowed down to about 3,000 soldiers. The stability Afghans were experiencing was finally paying off. Americans overall don't understand this type of commitment. By remaining the U.S. Government and military could train more soldiers in Pashtu and the other ethnic languages of this region. Then, soldiers deployed to Afghanistan would have the opportunity to converse and get to know the Afghan citizens better. They would be able to find out firsthand the nuances between the Taliban, Sunnis, al-Qaida, ISIS and other extremist groups. If these groups are fighting with each other, a better comprehension of the history and root causes of these conflicts could be acquired through conversations with them in their native languages. This takes time and a total engagement from the U.S. The everyday American citizen would have to be committed as well.

In America churches of different denominations (Catholic, Baptist, Jewish and others) must discuss Islam and its meaning to gain a deeper sense of the faith that drives groups like the Taliban. Ministers should still preach from the Bible about the teachings of Jesus and the Torah, but the outside world, especially the countries adhering to Islam, must be included in their sermons and presentations of the gospel. Since people are taught to love their enemies, Americans must first begin by becoming more insightful about their enemies. If the Taliban are considered barbarians, why is this so? Are the Taliban fighters brainwashed to blame others outside of their *"circles"* as being infidels and thus subject them to death? What can Americans do to help change their perception among the Taliban and other extremist organizations? Do Americans only get involved with other countries to invade, destroy and steal their wealth, whether it be oil or land, and then impose their political philosophy on others? Are Americans too materialistic and not as religiously minded as other cultures to respect their pledge to Allah (God)? If Allah is God, why would He promote violence against members of other religious sects? Do democracy, materialism and consumerism represent forms of bloodshed towards others? These are questions Americans must ponder and ask themselves.

Rafael understood Americans and people from other developed countries did not know much about Afghanistan's history, culture and religion. According to Gilles Dorronsoro in his book *The Taliban's Winning Strategy in Afghanistan*, he points out that the Taliban is deeply opposed to the tribal structure in Afghanistan, and they promote *mullahs* (educated Muslims trained in religious law and doctrine) as main political leaders in the states they create. It is also known they are interconnected to the international *jihadist* movement and obtain political support by opposing foreign occupation. Their principal objective, like it was in the 1990s, is to take hold of Kabul to build an Islamic Emirate based on Sharia Law. In the North of Afghanistan, the Herb-i-Islami (an Islamic organization known for fighting the Soviet occupation of Afghanistan) can recruit from the non-Pashtun ethnic groups. The Taliban is centralized but very flexible when adapting to issues at a local level, and they are the most successful and effective guerrilla movement of the country's history.

Even though the Taliban fighters are not as technologically advanced as the international coalition (IC), they are very capable of using radios and cell phones to rally up large groups of fighters. They are also very mobile, and they are advancing their use of improvised explosive devices (IEDs). The fighters are very courageous, and they have a very strong ideological commitment to the war. They effectively use propaganda to gain the support of the population by highlighting through their media outlets the corruption of the Afghan Government, the lack of basic services for the people and the cultural narrative of the struggle against the infidel invaders (British, Soviets and Americans). The support for the Taliban by Pashtuns in rural areas is very favorable among the *mullahs* and fundamentalists. The Uzbecks and Turkmen generally abhor and do not support the Taliban, and neither do the educated urban Afghans nor the Shi'a back the Taliban.

The U.S. military establishment and American politicos are generally unaware of the cultural insights of Afghan society or any country, outside of the U.S., for that matter. By neglecting and ignoring Afghan history and its ethnic diversity, the U.S. and the IC forces are already at a huge disadvantage in the war they initiated after the 9/11 attacks of 2001. The Pashtuns, for example, are the most numerous ethnic group (40 percent of the population), and they are alienated by the central government. They believe the government is influenced primarily by non-Pashtun leaders since 2001. Hamid Karzai, the former president of Afghanistan, is from an aristocratic family from Kandahar, but he is viewed as being a puppet of the U.S. Conversely, the non-Pashtuns resent the favoritism directed towards the Pashtuns who supposedly benefit the most from the bulk of international money received. On top of this, the state is very weak, lacks neutrality and is incapable of arbitrating disputes. Foreign countries also are suspected of having their own agendas. For example, Turkey exclusively supports the Uzbecks and Turkmen by providing protection to Rashid Dostum, the leader of the Jumbesh Party. To further exacerbate the problem, more than 10,000 foreigners, who mostly live in Kabul, are separated from the Afghan people and thus live a lavish lifestyle in comparison to the general population. Foreigners also earn huge salaries and don't pay taxes; the majority of them do not learn a local language.

Again, Rafael and Josefina could ascertain this separation among the foreigners of the U.S. and other countries from the locals was evident in Kabul. American society was built on the segregation of ethnic groups (Blacks, Whites, Hispanics and others) as it is represented throughout the U.S. enclaves of the country. In addition, most people from rural communities do not venture outside of their small towns, for the most part, and they do not travel beyond the borders of the U.S. This spawns a type of isolation from others and oneself. It is almost the responsibility of all people to travel and break past the known boundaries that are familiar to them. Once a person lives within his own box, he becomes subject to the "brainwashing" provided by the media, whether it be CNN, Fox News or any other informational network. This detachment in America and other countries of the world foments a distrust, and it actually goes against the grain of what it is to be human. A person's life here on earth is limited, and his time should be spent exploring and learning about others. This is the true "art of balancing" because when he does this, he also learns about himself. Rafael didn't want to be like so many elderly people who only eat, watch T.V., visit the same family members and friends, go to the same church and, basically, repeat this routine for the remainder of their lives. There is not just one town in each state of America, and there is not just one state in the nation. The U.S. doesn't exist solely by itself in the world because there is a plethora of countries and cultures throughout the global community. Americans are part of this extensive puzzle just as the French, Germans, Spanish, Russians, Asians, Hispanics and others are. If the world consisted of just one town, one state and one country, isolationism would make sense. But this is not the case.

GOYA'S DARK GENIUS

LATE ONE AFTERNOON after a hot and windy 54-mile bike ride, Rafael sat in front of his computer to write some before Josefina returned from a full day of work. His mind shifted to Francisco de Goya, one of the most outstanding and laudable *art virtuososs* of the world. Goya was born on March 30, 1746 in Fuendetodos, Spain. He grew up in poverty even though his mother of noble descent owned some land. His father was an average gilder who socialized with other artisans and anonymous artists. His family lived in Zaragoza, and the young Goya attended *Escuelas Pías*, which was a Piarist school founded by the Aragonese priest José Calasanz in the seventeenth century. This was a religious institution originally established in Rome. From there, Goya attended the studio of José Luzán, a local painter, in 1760. Luzán had worked in Italy, and he preferred the Baroque style. It must be underscored that Goya opposed the conventions of the times. Going against the rules and dogmas instituted by academia, he defended his claim that "there are no rules in painting." This is significant to point out because art, like any form of creative endeavor, should not be confined to anyone's standards. This type of limitation evokes the repetition of certain themes over and over again.

In 1792 Goya went to Cádiz where he became extremely ill, and he stayed in the home of Sebastián Martínez, a friend who was a wealthy trader. It is not known exactly what he suffered from, but he was paralyzed for a short period and became permanently deaf. He also experienced a lot of pain and heard noises in his head. During this period of his life, he chose to paint works that were not commissioned; as a result, he was able to express the "pure expression" of a concept or idea. The paradox of his works ranged from a religious and mystical painter to one that also depicted the horrors of France invading Spain in 1808 and the Spanish Revolution between Liberals and Conservatives in the 1820s (known as his Black Paintings). It is imperative to take notice of the stark contrast of Goya's dark paintings when compared to his previous work. Goya moved into *Quinta del Sordo* (House of the Deaf Man) in 1819, which was located on the outskirts of Madrid.

Although *Saturn Devouring His Son* is Goya's most well-known work of his dark period, Rafael thought about the meaning of *The Fates*. It is documented that in classical mythology the Fates are three goddesses who control the timeline of life. They symbolize destiny or fate. Clotho, the first one, is in charge of spinning the thread of life, and Lachesis, the second one, controls the period between birth and death while Atropos, the third one, cuts the cord (representative of death). In the classical depiction, Clotho holds a spool, Lachesis clutches the thread coming from it, and Atropos cuts the strand with shears. On the other hand, Goya depicts Clotho grasping an effigy, Lachesis has a looking-glass lens and Atropos holds small scissors. Between these goddesses a man is painted holding them as he is suspended in the air. Rafael interpreted this as Goya reviewing his life now that he was deaf and ill. It takes courage for a person to exam and process his own death, which is frightening and dark. As an artist Goya was also very sensitive to the wars and their effects on the Spanish people and himself. He was also enduring the death of his wife. There is no doubt this painting is a reflection of his dreams and unconscious mind.

The breadth and depth of Goya's work is exceptional because there were few, if any artist during the nineteenth century, who explored so many concepts. By filling *Quinta del Sordo* with these dark creations, he was surrounding himself with these morbid thoughts expressed in the *diptychs* of witches, the "goat man" and the grotesqueness of *Saturn Devouring His Son*. Basically, he was facing his own demons as man is forced to do at some point or another along the course of his life. This process is risky and painful, and one that many times a person chooses to ignore. This juxtaposition of life and death was also delineated in Goya's paintings of the bullfighter fighting the bull with the potential of the beast killing the man. The *matador* facing the raging bull is apposed with Goya's realization of his own fate with the forceful strokes of his paintbrush immersed in dark colors (gold and black). He confronted the mystery and horror of death, one accentuated more emphatically by his deafness and sounds bouncing around in his head. His artwork served as a creative outlet for cathartically releasing his fears and anxieties regarding the fine line between life and death.

It's the balance Goya was probably seeking, in separating himself in his new home on the outskirts of Madrid, to rest, meditate and take action by means of his work. *The Fates* is actually the "fate" of all humans. Individually, a person is tasked with contemplating his life from nascence to his demise. Lachesis with her lens examines the man's life held in a suspended state. Lachesis could be God's representative reviewing each individual life on earth as well as man reflecting upon his own personal existence. There is an interconnectedness here between the enigma and delightful astonishment of living and the filament that delicately holds life and death together. Like the doctor cutting the umbilical cord at inception, separating the baby from his mother, each person is severed from the life he has lived to enter the unknown chambers of the afterlife where the physical being metamorphosizes into the spiritual realm (a new form of creation and being). Rafael believed that meditating on mortality can become an illuminating, meaningful and peaceful mechanism for man to consider, or it can be a lurid and terrifying experience if he willfully chooses to *slight* it and keep it at bay in the undisclosed chambers of his unconscious mind, which can flood a person with nightmarish and disturbing anxieties. As someone viewing *The Fates*, Goya challenges each person patently to take this dichotomy between living and perishing and the in-between to heart. Is this individual able to reflect upon the inevitable destiny and fate that awaits him and all of humanity?

SPORTS, POLITICS AND THE ART OF WAR

ART AND SPORTS teach mankind a lot about life. As Josefina and Rafael watched the U.S. Open Tennis Championships in New York this past Sunday between Novak Djokovic and Daniil Medvedev, Rafael was surprised to see Novak crush his racket after several missed points in the second set. If he were to win this tournament, Djokovic would have claimed 21 Grand Slam titles beating the record of 20, he now shares with Rafael Nadal and Roger Federer. By dominating the U.S. Open, he would have also captured four major championships in one year, a feat that only five single players have done. Rafael learned that Novak has a history of losing his temper and breaking his racket as he did during the Olympic Games in Tokyo 2021. Not only did he destroy his racket, but he also threw it into the empty stands. It seems like this display of anger should not be tolerated at the professional level of tennis. Athletes should conduct themselves in a courteous and respectful manner on the court while performing in front of the world. Yes, he is a human being, and sometimes a person's emotions get the best of him. But this is about Novak, one of the richest and greatest tennis players of all time. When a player like him loses, he should know better than anyone else that someone is always going to win while the other person, and the opponent in this case, loses. Defeat is part of being a winner and a great athlete. But by violently breaking and throwing a racket, the athlete is forgetting what the sport is all about. Maybe society and its attitudes about winning and losing are affecting many professional players in many sport arenas.

Djokovic failed to embrace the precepts and maxims of Sun Tzu revealed in his book *The Art of War*. One of the main golden nuggets of his philosophy is to know yourself and know your enemy or opponent, which in this case is tennis and sports. There is a time to retreat as well as a time to attack. When Djokovic smashed his racket because things weren't going his way, he allowed his opponent to capture the upper hand by continuing his aggressive play at a moment of vulnerability displayed by Novak. A person generally is cognizant of events in his life that are not always going to go his way. As a result, it is essential to remain calm, breathe and collect yourself, acknowledging it is about the process, not the final result. By focusing just on victory, a person loses sight of the goal at hand. It is the moment to moment reaction to adversity or success that determines the outcome. The opposite of war is peace, and the flipside of defeat is victory. There will be many losses in life accompanied by triumphs.

President Biden and Secretary of State Anthony Blinken failed to observe and practice Tzu's concepts when withdrawing from Afghanistan on August 31, 2021. From a position of strength, they quickly retreated to one of weakness. They along with previous American administrations did not clearly define the goal of their invasion of Afghanistan after the attacks of September 11, 2001. David French, a senior editor at the *Dispatch* and columnist for *Time*, points out this mistake in his article "American Leaders Made Defeat in Afghanistan Inevitable." This past week America remembered the anniversary of the 9/11 attacks twenty years ago. The president and secretary of state *flopped* to mention there has not been an attack of this magnitude since then on American soil. Furthermore, the American and coalition forces have assisted the Afghan military at keeping the Taliban and al-Qaida at bay with a minimum contingency of American soldiers in Afghanistan. Most importantly, millions of Afghans, especially women, lived free from the control and medieval "enslavement" of the Taliban. This is the vision

Biden and Trump should have repeatedly expressed to the American people. Trump referred to the war in Afghanistan as an "endless war," and Biden wanted to withdraw because his administration was "not willing to enter a third decade of conflict."

The key words here used by these presidents are "war" and "conflict." If a person takes into account the opposite meaning of these articulations, he finds "peace" and "stability." This is what the American and IC have achieved over the past twenty years. It is easy to forget the Taliban and its allies are fighting a religious war. It's a cultural concept, which is difficult for the American administration and public to comprehend. This idea of *jihad* cannot ever be erased, but it can be contained and kept at bay as the U.S. has done over the past twenty years. Just as the U.S. has retained forces in Germany, South Korea and other parts of the world, America should have kept a small military detachment in Afghanistan. The only American military fatalities in the past year occurred during the hasty and unorganized withdrawal by the U.S. from Kabul just a few weeks ago. However, the sacrifices and lost lives of the men and women who served, not only as members of the American and coalition forces but also of the Afghan Army, which numbers about 50,000 dead, have been in vein. The Taliban and its allies knew something about the U.S., which Americans didn't know about themselves; that is the American resolve to fight would eventually wane, and they would withdraw. This is exactly what happened, and this is why the Taliban was victorious.

The art of balancing requires man to find the equilibrium in a complex world of opposites and their counterparts: war and peace, hate and love, courage and cowardice, light and darkness, happiness and sadness and many other combinations. As Tzu reminds humankind, "The true object of war is peace." Man is at war with himself and with his neighbor locally and abroad. To learn about others beyond our American definition, a person must learn their language, culture, traditions and history after knowing his own language, culture and history. Man must not isolate himself within the confines only of his *milieu* and of what is known to him. He must venture out into unknown places where "conflict" is waiting in order to meet it head on. At times, force is needed, for example, when the U.S. killed Osama Bin Laden, the author of the 9/11 attacks. But after strength is expressed, it's necessary to realize that maintaining peace is a constant battle; it's one that must be forged by being involved and not withdrawing. America cannot dig and hide under a rock and pretend conflicts and wars will go away with deep meditation, profound breathing and positive thinking. However, these tools for relaxing the American spirit are important and necessary to implement in a world where tensions will always exist discretely and globally. Once this is espoused and practiced, Americans as a nation with competent leaders can begin to realize peace among nations is only accomplished by redefining war as Tzu would have a person do. The wise result of this type of comprehensive contention is everlasting peace in which dissensions are championed and from which countries are not disengaged.

RELIGIOUS SERVICES LACK SUSTENANCE

IT WAS SUNDAY, and Rafael and Josefina returned from Mass at Josefina's Catholic Church. They would usually alternate between her church and a nondenominational one Rafael enjoyed and felt like he received a good and worthwhile message. Attending the Catholic Mass three Sundays in a row was almost blasphemy in Rafael's mind. No emotion was read into the three scriptures before the homily, which was mindlessly uttered and was exactly the complete repetition of the sacred writings just read. No thorough insight or speculation was provided. What would Jesus say about a service that does not engage the congregation and is indifferent to societal issues and each person there? It was completely torturous to participate in a Mass that never modified from the norm. Rafael attended only because God was important to him and his relationship with Josefina. But he could see why so many had left the Catholic Church. In his mind it was dead, and it was a shame because the Bible is so rich and full of wisdom. Maybe the Church has become so big and dogmatic that it was impossible to divert its course. It was out of step with society and the younger generation needing to be exposed to a more energetic and contemporary liturgy. The Indian father spoke broken English, but that wasn't the problem. There was no inquisitiveness in his speech. There was no interjection about his civilization or traditions in India, and he offered no insight into the readings he had done during his seminary studies to pepper his homely. There was a void going to Mass, and Rafael watched others as if they were resigned and obligated by faith to endure such monotony and dreadfulness.

All people should be exposed to philosophy since it afforded a person the opportunity to think and reflect upon the ideas and maxims of others. What is the purpose of life? It is probably the most important question that every person must ask himself. This year has been especially challenging for Rafael since he had not been able to travel to Europe or to another country he had yet to visit. It seemed like peregrinating was crucial for awakening the continued curiosity individuals must keep fresh as responsible members of the world. Talking to people, who don't read, travel or ask questions, was extremely boring to Rafael. People have a tendency to repeat the same routines over and over again. It's like going to the gym and working out while observing the same members there every time. Today, at the gym, Rafael greeted Carlos who does the same incline bench movement once or twice a week. It's the only exercise he does. They just nodded at one another to acknowledge each other's presence. No words were exchanged, just a bob of heads as each one returned to his *groove*. Fox News indoctrinate people on the Right, and CNN brainwashes people on the Left. America is divided, and people respectively are living their separate lives.

Spiritually, society is living in an abyss where there is no communication. People are not interested in one another, and few want to learn about others. Socrates coined the overused phrase: "Know thyself." He truly wanted a person to know his true passions, but he also implied that man must understand others. However, in American society a person learns to be independent, and he only comes together with others in meetings at work, church or concerts, for example, because that is the *touchstone* for gatherings. Once the meeting is concluded, each individual goes his separate way and does his own thing. Family members don't impart new ideas about compulsory issues. A sister-in-law may sit at a table where a newly published book has been written by its author, her brother-in-law who is present, but she completely scorns it because she is afraid to engage in a dialogue, whether it be political, cultural or spiritual. Each person seems to be out of balance with himself and his surroundings. People attend weddings to watch others and to observe and critique what each person is wearing. There is no true interest in conversing unless someone asks all the questions and the other person answers them as quickly as possible in order to return to his smartphone to post a picture on social media. People want to be loved, but they don't know how to love others. An artist, for example, is only interested in his work and avoids the accomplishments of others. He'll talk endless about what he has achieved and what he is working on without, that's right, asking others about their projects. Many people just live aimlessly doing chores: cleaning and remodeling their homes, running to the coffee shop and talking indiscriminately with friends and family members about the latest Netflix movie or the most recent clip from TED Talks they've watched.

THE ART OF BALANCING IN AN INATTENTIVE AND DIVIDED WORLD

PEOPLE WANT TO be heard, but they don't want to listen to others. This is the pretext for living in a divided society where its populace just doesn't get along. This state of unbalanced living is stressful and alienating. The recent crisis at the Texas border, where thousands of migrants from Haiti, Central America and other third-world countries swarmed to the *Río Grande* separating the cities of Del Río and Ciudad Acuña, is representative of the oppressive diplomacy the U.S. and other countries like France have exercised on these nations. The U.S. could be directly faulted by the exploits of the United Fruit Company in the early to mid-twentieth century for exploiting countries like Guatemala, Honduras and El Salvador by establishing puppet dictators and creating commercial bonds between the elite of those countries and the U.S. businesses in which the poor, those who flock to the borders today, where forced to work in the banana, sugar and coffee fields in those Central American countries for a meager paycheck. When Haiti gained its independence from the colonial grip of the French in the early nineteenth century, the French elite on the island and the countrymen at home were infuriated. The French were going to reinvade the country with its rich and fertile soil very conducive for the production of sugar unless the Haitians agreed to pay millions of francs in order to retain their independence. They knew this would cripple the Haitians since they would have to take out loans with high interest rates that would further have them collapse into the economic abyss of debt and poverty. Today, both the Democrats and Republicans are at their wits' end as to how to proceed to address the immigration problem. The recent earthquake in Haiti along with the recent assassination of its president only adds to the complexities the U.S. helped to create.

The answer to these complex issues must begin with the "art of balancing" in a man's individual existence and the collective lives of society's members. Americans must live more humbly and meekly as God would want them to do. By investing less in our homes and personal needs, Americans must begin to learn about the histories of other countries like Haiti, Afghanistan, Mexico and basically all the countries all over the globe, but especially those in close proximity to their borders and in their geographical hemisphere. Schools must provide a more rigorous curriculum for foreign languages, especially Spanish if living in the Southwest, and history, not only of the U.S., but also of those countries to the south and north and all over the world. Technology, science and math should be taught as well, but these subjects have been given a higher priority over the "soft" subjects previously mentioned. The lack of cultured individuals in America is a reflection of its elected officials. Former President Trump was steeped in his desire to "Make America Great" by promoting the wealth of Americans at the expense of the Third World countries.. President Biden and Liberal Democrats resolve to steal from the rich to pay for the deficiencies of society. Biden could not comprehend the failure of pulling out of Afghanistan in such a cowardly manner, leaving behind many Americans and Afghan women and children who will be abused and killed under the rule of the Taliban. The current administration like past ones lack the "cultural muscle" to navigate the complexities and nuances of a diverse world.

Rafael realized that "balancing" is not just a physical act of maintaining your equilibrium on a bicycle, but it is also an individual and collective act of spiritual and national responsibility to one another at home and throughout the world's community. The numbness he felt in his upper lip due to the initial impact of his face against the asphalt and the subsequent surgeries reminded him that setbacks allow a person to examine his life subjectively and holistically. It's the responsibility of each individual to dialogue with himself and others to reach a better understanding of their purpose here on earth. Much like the five fingers of a hand, men and women must work together because, as humans with intricate body parts and functions, they are cut from the same cloth in the same-shared world. Rafael's purpose was to write and contemplate his own views of himself in his life here and abroad. He would not settle for accepting the maxims, intellectual observations or philosophies of some other savant, such as Voltaire, Emerson, Kant or others, who came before him. Furthermore, he knew it was essentially indispensable to read the ideas and teachings of others, as an intellectual springboard, for stringing together his own path to walk on during his limited time here on earth. His spiritual need to trust God and search for *tranquil waters* in the midst of quagmires of chaos and confusion was also very significant for his well-being. Conversely, he knew it was necessary to question the unexamined concepts of many churches and religions stagnated by the dogma of tradition. Many theologians separated themselves in their power, palaces and repetition of mindless conventions and scriptural interpretations that did not challenge their parishioners to think for themselves. Corrupt governments throughout the world coexisted with these nonsensical religious and dogmatic leaders and entities. What would Jesus say?

Writing for Rafael was a form of meditation. He was not so concerned about succumbing to the publishing world and of spending hundreds of dollars to market his books, but his true purpose was to discourse with himself even if others never read his work. He'll never forget the individuals who disdained his book, which was sitting on the dining room table of their home. many years ago. The two people were members of his family in which there usually exists a cohesive exchange of support and dialogue. He was not bitter by this lack of interest in others, but it did *crystalize* in his mind how difficult it is for people to reach out and show a genuine interest in their fellow human beings. He was not discouraged, but he became more motivated to continue his solitary journey unnoticed in a society and world drowning in its old self-inflicted deception. He did not consider this a collective judgement but rather a reality he noticed in his experiences with others. It wasn't so much that some people didn't read his books; but, mainly, they did not have more profound conversations and discourses with one another. In various civilized communities, a person is more impressed and interested in the exterior of a home and its meticulous landscape than he is in the content of someone's heart and soul. Going to a gym, for example, where the majority of people are more interested in looking at themselves in a mirror and recording their routines on video with smart phones than they are observing or talking to others beyond themselves or their inner circle of acquaintances. Social media is another tool that allows people to photograph their cosmetic faces and bodies for others to envy and post their views on politics and religion without having the face-to-face verbal exchange with another warmhearted being. These actions lead to the disequilibrium of someone's individual self from others in which each person remains in a deplorable state of separateness. It is the emotional and spiritual pandemic of the current tumultuous times. No wonder many are experiencing more pain than joy in their lives.

For Rafael the existential art of balancing theme came to mind that early December afternoon in 2019 when he slid into the patch of gravel on his bike landing on the left side of his face. It was a reminder that things happen and serve as a *wake-up call* forcing a person to re-examine the purpose of his life. This led Rafael to think of the biblical Joshua, the prophet who led the twelve tribes of Israel across the Jordan Sea. The Ark of God was carried first as the water was split in half for their crossing. Twelve stones were laid in the middle of the parted sea, and twelve others were placed on the land where they came ashore. Once they crossed, the water covered the first set of stones whereas the others are still visible on the shore today. Man is reminded God is the miracle worker, and many times a sentient mortal cannot see his presence just as those natural symbols placed underwater are not discernible now. It represents man's soul, which is nourished by God's ubiquity. The exterior world is also a testament of His grace since everything is always in balance. The sun rises each morning in the East and sets each evening in the West. Man is awakened by the first song of the birds at dawn, and the moon and stars assure him of God's constant presence at night.

Death forces man to acknowledge the brevity of life. At times, he may think he will live forever, especially during his younger years. The falls and tumbles of life force him to reconsider what is essential. Meditation and prayer are required for establishing a relationship with God since man only sequesters himself in a whirlwind of bewilderment without his guiding light. Exercise is necessary for aging gracefully and keeping his body at its best, knowing each year he inches closer to death. Physical exertion, for the most part, leads to good health, and this increases man's ability to live a happy and less stressful life. Traveling to other countries, learning another language and listening to others utter in foreign tongues, he doesn't understand, help him realize he is part of a diverse tapestry in an ever changing, divergent and global milieu. It is refreshing and rejuvenating for a person to go abroad to expose himself to unknown cultures and civilizations. Reading gives him the opportunity to sit quietly and listen to the thoughts and ideas of others. The silent cerebral exchange of a reader with the written word green-lights him to ponder a new idea and see this thought chiseled with the permanence of ink on the page and expressed in a unique way. Writing, especially for Rafael, gives him the space to reflect on his love for Josefina, family and for all that life offers.

FINAL RUMINATION

GRATEFULNESS IS THE noun that best describes Rafael's journey in redacting this manuscript. He is thankful for his experience of growing up in Puerto Rico and of now living in Texas for approximately 48 years. He is also appreciative for the fortuitousness, time and money to be able to travel quite extensively throughout the Caribbean, Europe, Mexico, Central and Latin America and other parts of the globe. Rafael's educational background also afforded him the curiosity necessary to explore the classics from Plato, Schopenhauer, Voltaire and many others. Voltaire's *signature idea* underscored in Candide of cultivating a person's own garden is one Rafael feels is crucial for every individual alive because living is a process man has to figure out and experience for himself. Each person on this planet is a unique human being with different talents. This thought is further emphasized by Plato who stated: "The due proportion of mind and body is the loveliest and fairest sight to him who has a seeing eye." The concept of equilibrium is something man has to contemplate in this existential journey called *experiential sentience.* The pen is the tool Rafael uses to expose the "seeds" of unseen thoughts bursting to blossom on the garden's page, creating a symphony of colors, sounds and sights, for nourishing the soul's need for an appetite of tropes and images revealed by the author seeking this *equipoise* to honor and revere his *Essential Breath* for living in his immediate and faraway surroundings.